We Remember When

We Remember When

A Collection of Memoirs Written by Residents of

Fuller Village

in

Milton, Massachusetts

ISBN 978-0-557-94472-9

ACKNOWLEDGMENTS

By Betsy Buchbinder
Memoir Committee Chair

I want to take this opportunity to express my profound gratitude to an extraordinary group of people: the Fuller Village Memoir Committee. The committee is comprised of Fuller Village residents John Driscoll, Blossom Glassman, Nancy Kearns, Thomas O'Connor, Elaine Pinderhughes, Michael Ryan, and Ellen White. Each of these individuals has given generously of their unique skills and expertise to this project.

Everlasting thanks to Michael Ryan, who formatted all of the memoirs, photographed the authors, and served as our liaison with the publisher and as diplomat without peer.

Sincere appreciation to our consultant Dr. Katie Conboy, Provost and Vice President for Academic Affairs, Stonehill College, whose initial guidance helped to set the goals and standards we have followed.

And our everlasting gratitude to syndicated columnist and author Suzette Martinez Standring, who conducted writing workshops for our residents and who inspired even the most reluctant resident to share significant moments and memories in their lives.

Thanks to Deborah Felton, Executive Director of Fuller Village, for her support and encouragement of this memoir project. We are grateful as well to Fuller Village Activities Director Lisa Coover for the publicity she afforded us, and to Muriel Pellegrino for her typing skills.

We Remember When: growing up, sadness and joy, travel, the perils and pain of war, finding love, suffering loss, trials and tribulations, life's lessons, surviving and overcoming, helping and being helped, foreign intrigue, and unintended consequences.

The infinite variety of human experiences is here in this collection of memoirs; it is all here in this unique book of remembrances.

The Memoir Committee

(L to R) Betsy Buchbinder, John Driscoll
Elaine Pinderhughes, Michael Ryan

(L to R) Ellen White, Thomas O'Connor
Blossom Glassman, Nancy Kearns

Historic Election

John T. Driscoll

On November 8, 1960, Jean and I sat up in bed and watched what was to become one of the most famous U.S. election nights ever—Republican Vice President Richard M. Nixon vs. Democratic U. S. Senator John F. Kennedy.

We saw that election process evolve all through the night until at least 3:00 AM—and it hadn't finished at that point. Actually, the Kennedy-Nixon race was so close that it went into the following morning. Then about 7:00 AM, there finally was a declared winner—John Fitzgerald Kennedy, with 49.7 percent of the popular vote to Richard Nixon's 49.6 percent! It was the closest popular vote margin in the twentieth century! But the key to the election was the electoral vote: Kennedy 303/Nixon 219. Nixon didn't concede his defeat until the afternoon of November 9.

Following Jack's victory, Jean and I, and my brother Bill and his wife, Mary, and a few other friends, set off on a planned trip down to Florida for a well-deserved vacation. However, before I left I wrote the president-elect a note, congratulating him, and telling him how pleased I was for him and for our country.

I received a nice note back from him, expressing his regret that he couldn't be in touch with me at that time. (Obviously he had plenty of work to attend to, including the organization of his cabinet.)

While we were in Florida, we drove by his house in Palm Beach. Our wives were anxious to see the Kennedy home—hoping against hope that they would run into him. Again as luck would have it, just as we drove by, he was coming out from the house and getting into a car in front of his home. The girls yelled to me, "Stop! Stop!" I said, "No, I really don't think it would be appropriate for us to stop and bother him. Whatever he's doing, it is a different scene now. He's the president-elect, and I don't want to interfere in that way." We drove on—and of course the ladies understood.

Jean and I, and my brother Bill, and his wife, Mary, were invited to President-Elect John F. Kennedy's inaugural swearing-in ceremony on the steps of the capitol. It was January 20, 1961. It was a few days after my own inauguration at the state house in January, when I was sworn in as Treasurer of the Commonwealth of Massachusetts.

That night, Jean and I and Bill and Mary drove down to Washington, DC, and began attending various events—parties, inaugural balls—leading up to the president's inauguration. We had exceptionally good seats, both at the inauguration and for Kennedy's famous "New Frontier" speech: "Ask not what your country can do for you. Ask what you can do for your country!"

We were in the presidential parade viewing grandstand directly across the street from the White House. The presidential reviewing stand—with John Fitzgerald Kennedy, his wife, Jacqueline, and their parents, plus Democratic Party and world leaders—was situated on the White House lawn looking out onto Pennsylvania Avenue. We were directly across from them, so we also had a complete view of the parade and the presidential party.

After that, I had a few visits to the White House during Jack Kennedy's "Thousand Days" as president of the United States. One visit that comes to mind was when he was pinning medals on three of the astronauts who had just returned from one of their missions—and he didn't know I was there. As they were leaving the Rose Garden, escorting the astronauts to the front entrance to the White House, the president spotted me standing along the edge of the sidewalk that comes from the Oval Office toward the back of the building. I had two guests with me. He stopped the little parade of people and came right over and told me he was surprised to see me there. He didn't know I was coming. Of course, I didn't know I was going to go there either, simply because I was in Washington at the Pentagon on business. With me were Larry Sullivan, one of my deputy treasurers, and Jimmy Linehan, a CPA who was doing work for me with the state.

I happened to call over to the White House, and I spoke with Kenny O'Donnell, the special assistant to the president. He invited the three of us to come to the medal ceremony. And as luck would have it, the president stopped by and greeted us. We were thrilled!

Our last visit was probably the single most important one! It was October 25, 1963, and I had been asked by the United Fund of Massachusetts to go down to Washington to try to get a donation from President Kennedy for the fund. At that time, I was the state chairman for the government division of the United Fund. The leadership of the United Fund knew that I was a friend of President Kennedy. So they asked me if I would go down and get a donation from him.

So we set it up for October 25, through Kenny O'Donnell, and Jean went with me. When we went into the White House Oval Office, the official photographer was there. And while the president and I were posing and talking, he handed me a $500 check, and asked, "John, you're head of the government division of the United Fund, but who is the general chairman of the United Fund?" I answered, "Elliot Richardson." Then, with a big smile on his face, he said: "And you want me to give my money to that son-of-a-bleep?" [Elliot Richardson was a Yankee Republican, who JFK had removed as U. S. Attorney for Massachusetts (1959–61), because he wanted a Democrat, Arthur Garrity, whom he appointed. Later, Richardson became Massachusetts lieutenant governor (1965–67) and then attorney general (1967–69).]

Well, we had a big laugh, and the photographer snapped that picture. Then the president invited Jean to come over and have her picture taken with him, and with me. Jean in her own shy way just said, "Thank you, Mr. President, John's here on business, and I'm just tagging along, so I don't want to interfere." To which the president replied, "Never mind business, or talking about tagging along, I'd like to have you in the picture with us."

That picture is hanging in my den, in my condo in Milton. It was taken in the Oval Office on Friday, October 25, 1963—one month before President Kennedy was assassinated on Friday, November 22.

We were very fortunate to have been there with President Kennedy in those final days of his life! We left the White House that day, very pleased to have been able to visit the president of the United States, grateful for his United Fund donation, and very happy about our little reunion meeting. Jean was truly fond of him, as was I. I believe we had a really genuine friendship with him. One month later, he was assassinated, and the whole world stopped still—and particularly mine and Jean's world!

But, I was lucky enough to have that picture sent to me—probably by his secretary Evelyn Lincoln—considering all of the concern and commotion following the assassination.

I went to Washington on a National Guard plane, along with all of the other Massachusetts Constitutional Office holders, and certain other Massachusetts dignitaries. We were invited down to participate in the funeral service and view JFK's casket in the rotunda of the capitol building.

I spent some lonely days down there over that weekend on Saturday and Sunday. Monday was the funeral. I did the rotunda viewing with U. S. Congressman Eddie Boland (D-Springfield), who made it possible for me to come into the rotunda through the Congressional entrance, as opposed to standing in a very long line. I don't know how many thousands of mourners were standing in line. Later, the casket was moved from the rotunda to the East Room of the White House for a private mourning, to which I, along with the rest of the Massachusetts delegation, was invited.

Those were very long and sad days after the president of the United States—with so much charisma, and so much to offer, as did his wife Jacqueline—had his young life senselessly taken from the American people—and from us!

It was very lonely, and I can remember crying on the telephone as I talked to Jean, who was attending to different duties on that Sunday—being a godmother for one of Dave and Mary Jane Murray's children.

Legacy File

Mae Thomas Evangelista

It was a cold September evening. Our son, Tony, two years and a few months old, was sitting on my lap half asleep. He said, "Mommy, when will I have my two baby sisters?" I had to smile because our son would always pat my tummy and say I would bring him two baby sisters.

My husband, also named Tony, and I really expected that my second pregnancy would give us another *big* boy because that is what my doctor, Dr. Cola, would say when he examined me. "Mae, your baby has a very strong heartbeat; you are going to have a big baby boy."

September 26 was my due date, but nothing happened. Then two days later, I started to experience labor pains, and Tony took me to the hospital. After a while, I was out. It was 2:00 AM on September 29 when I awoke and pushed the call button for the nurse. When she arrived, I asked her if I had my baby. She smiled and said, "I cannot believe you do not remember. You had two beautiful baby girls, five pounds three and a half ounces and six pounds six ounces, and they were three minutes apart."

Wow, shock does not describe my reaction. What a blessed surprise. My husband and I asked Dr. Cola why he did not know I was carrying twins. He said that our babies were back-to-back, and he could only hear one strong heartbeat. He was as surprised as we were and said that my husband almost passed out when he told him the news.

Why, during all those months while I was pregnant, did my son keep saying he was going to have "two" baby sisters? Oh, and by the way, they were born on my birthday.

Halcyon Days

Ellen White

It was the summer of 1961. Schooling completed, my husband, Tom, and I were thinking about where we would settle down and spend the next fifty years. I, of course, loved New England, but he was from Florida and wanted to live there. We thought we would not make any decision but instead spend a year either traveling or living in New York City. We both loved music and the theater and decided to spend some time in Manhattan.

We found jobs—he at a hospital, and I at a broadcasting company. We rented a small apartment on the Upper West Side. It was a walk-up with one large room. On one side, there was a dining room table and chairs, and on the other side a pullout bed.

Although New York City is a widespread metropolis, like most cities it is made up of many neighborhoods. A half block away from our apartment was the small convenience store where we could buy the Sunday *New York Times* at the crack of dawn. Near the same corner were a pharmacy, a barbershop, shoe repair, and cleaners. Most of the owners knew the "regulars" and would greet the customers with a welcoming word—not much different from living in a small town.

There are theaters all over Manhattan. We saw Tennessee Williams' s *Streetcar Named Desire*, Checkhov's *The Cherry Orchard*, Arthur Miller's *All My Sons*, Eugene O'Neill's *Long Day's Journey into Night*, Henrik Ibsen's *Hedda Gabler,* and *The Caretaker* by Harold Pinter. For the theaters we frequented, we usually found a nearby restaurant we liked. Tom and I would meet at the restaurant after work and then go on to the theater.

This was many years before Lincoln Center was built. Operas were held in a beautiful old building on Broadway where one opera we attended featured Richard Tucker singing the lead. Chamber music recitals were held at various locations throughout the city. Leonard Bernstein had recently become the principal conductor of the New York Philharmonic, and we were fortunate to see him many evenings at Carnegie Hall.

The evenings I enjoyed the most were when we attended the theater on Broadway. We bought a book of tickets, allowing us to attend many preopening productions. *I Can Get It for You Wholesale* starred a little-known singer by the name of Barbara Streisand. The cast of *How to Succeed in Business* included a local boy, Robert Morse. We saw one of Jerry Herman's first plays, a musical entitled *Milk and Honey*. He went on to do *Hello Dolly*, *Mame,* and *La Cage aux Folles*. One Sunday afternoon, we went to see *The Fantastics,* which, at the time, was the longest running musical in history. *Gypsy,* with Ethel Merman, was still playing. Stephen Sondheim, who had written the lyrics to *West Side Story* a few years earlier, was back writing both words and music for *A Funny Thing Happened on the Way to the Forum.*

There were many Shakespeare productions throughout the city. That summer was the first time *Shakespeare in the Park* was presented in Central Park.

Often while we were walking home at night, we would stop in at a piano bar where Don Shirley, the jazz pianist, was performing. He was a master as was the cellist who would sometimes accompany him. One Sunday we were bicycling in Central Park and passed two gentlemen leaning on their bikes and chatting. I recognized Mr. Shirley and was so excited I nearly rode right into a pedestrian. I still own many of Don Shirley's records—on 33 1/3 rpm of course.

We had friends in New York and New Jersey who would join us for dinner and a play. We would go away some weekends to Boston or across the Hudson to New Jersey. We put many miles on our little Volkswagen bug with its sunroof, but we were always happy to get home to our "pad" in Manhattan.

The year was finally over, and Tom found a "real" job. We were ready to settle down and have a family. One of the last plays we saw before we left was the musical *Salad Days*. It originally played in England and was quite successful, but it was a flop on Broadway. It played briefly at the Barbizon Hotel. I especially remember one of the lines in a song: "We won't say these are the happiest days, just the happiest days so far." How true!

About fifteen years later, we were driving through New York City on our way to Maine. We had our four children in an RV and decided to go by our old neighborhood. What a shock! The place had been transformed. Trees had been installed in planters along the sidewalk, all of the apartments had been updated, and outside our old place was a long green awning stretching out to the street.

By the front door, a uniformed doorman stood awaiting the arrival of another resident. Gentrified indeed.

Gemini

Saul Buchbinder

To this very day, every time NASA announces a space flight, I recall my own feelings of unease and apprehension about a much earlier space flight—NASA's Gemini Project.

The corporation I had founded, ELASCO (The Electronic Assembly Co.) manufactured DC power supplies for electronic devices. In the early 1960s, I was contacted by RCA (Radio Corporation of America) to develop a power supply for the Gemini Project, America's quest to reach outer space for a two-week flight. It soon became a personal challenge as I read and reread the specifications that had been sent to me: to design a five-volt power supply that would be at least 70 percent efficient. At that time, a five-volt DC power supply had never been made to achieve more than 50 percent efficiency. The five-volt supply was needed to power Gemini's vital communication system.

Another roadblock was the fact that there were specific parameters for temperature that could be tolerated in outer space. Space was a significant new frontier for our country and, at a personal level, for a company that wanted to be a part of this exciting challenge. What followed were countless sleepless nights and constant conferences with my staff concerning the specifications for the weight and size of the power supply we had been asked to design.

One of my consultants was a friend who lived out of state, and when he called one evening, I told him about the Gemini Project. At first, he too did not believe it was possible to meet the many parameters involved, especially the efficiency aspect. But a few days later, he called to suggest that I send him the "specs" so that he could have another engineer look them over. He knew of someone who he thought might be able to design such a power supply.

Two weeks later, I received a large envelope from my friend containing a schematic for a five-volt power supply that might actually be at least 70 percent efficient! Some of the other specifications had also been addressed. Actually, the power supply turned out to be 73 percent efficient! However, the size of the supply was questionable and remained for me to resolve. After many more sleepless nights, I found a workable solution! I was anxious to speak to the genius who had solved so many of the challenges. I asked my friend to put me in touch with the engineer who had been so creative in his thinking.

I was told that I would never be able to speak to him. It was a strange response. After many requests, I was finally told that the man was institutionalized and saw only a small circle of people. His technical and creative genius had remained intact, but, sadly, he was unable to cope with people.

Gemini went into outer space successfully, and with it, an ELASCO power supply. I have often wondered, whenever NASA announced further space trips, whether the spacecraft included any of the other fifty ELASCO power supplies NASA had purchased. How many times had I reached outer space, and did ELASCO eventually find its way to the moon? I'd like to believe it did.

What Happened!

Herbert Colcord

Less than a year out of high school, I was now lying flat on my stomach in the middle of the hedgerows in Normandy, France, with machine gun bullets flying inches above my head, and my friend, John Spurr, lying wounded beside me. My life as a U.S. combat soldier was about to end, but the constant threat of death would follow me for the rest of the war.

My story begins in January of 1944 in southwest England near the town of Penzance. The 175th Regiment of the 29th Division was preparing for the invasion of Europe. In the forbidding moors that covered the countryside, the days invariably were rainy. It was not a fun time. The training was intense, and time passed quickly. Soon we were on our way to Plymouth on the coast of the English Channel.

It was June 3, 1944. We were briefed about our role in the coming invasion of France. After sustained air and naval bombardment, the landing would supposedly take place at Normandy with minimal resistance from the enemy. Needless to say, this turned out to be a miscalculation! After the briefing, we had our last meal before boarding a ship for the voyage across the channel. It was not until after I returned home a year later that I learned much of the world was watching with great anticipation and hope. Millions were praying this would be the beginning of the end of World War II.

We started to cross the channel on June 4. However, the weather had other plans for us, and we were forced to return to port. On June 5 the sun came out, and we were again on our way in one long serpentine line of ships. The mood was somber as we suddenly realized this was the real thing. We would soon be on the shores of Omaha Beach in Normandy. We were actually sunning ourselves as we sliced through the water. My friend, John, who was twenty-five, suggested we attend a church service. I was eighteen and did not go with him. That decision bothered me for years after the war because John was killed in action and, for some reason, I was spared. In later years, I was able to resolve this situation in my own mind.

As we moved to our marshalling area about two miles off the coast of Omaha Beach, the sun was setting and the 116th Infantry Regiment was preparing for the initial assault that would take place at about 6:00 AM on D-Day—June 6. When we awakened from whatever sleep we could manage, the guns on the battleship USS *Texas* were firing shells at the Germans signaling the invasion was on.

Our responsibility at this point was to follow up the initial assault of the 116th Regiment. We did not know about the bloodshed those soldiers had suffered on the beach. As nighttime settled in and early morning arrived, we could see that the assault of the first day had not gone well. As we prepared to go over the side down the rope ladder to the Higgins boats, the wounded of the first day were being brought onto the ship from the other side. The trip down the rope ladder was precarious, as we had no previous training. We climbed onto the ladders, each carrying fifty pounds of equipment and a rifle, knowing that one misstep would result in a forty-foot fall. All of this took place in pitch-blackness. We had no idea what we were about to experience.

It was now early morning on June 7, 1944. We took off in the Higgins boats for the beach about 4:00 AM amid much shouting from the naval officer in charge. It was really chaotic. The ride to the beach was tense. Our destination was a sector named *Dog Red* at the eastern end of the beach. When we arrived at the halfway point, enemy resistance began to flare up on that beach, and the coxswain was ordered to change our destination to a sector named *Easy Green*. At that point, all of us—about thirty men or one platoon—were instructed to take our rifles off safety. If the mood was tense when we started, it was now filled with incredible anxiety! My biggest concern was hoping the coxswain would drive the boat close enough to shore, so I wouldn't have to swim—because I couldn't!

After we landed and moved inland a few hundred yards, we ran into some machine gun fire. We lost a few men to artillery fire, but the troops who landed before us had a much rougher time. There were bodies everywhere on the beach. I remember in particular the bodies of six medics lying side by side. As we moved up a path, we came across a signal outfit where one shell had killed five men severing the head of the lead wireman. Once we reached high ground, things quieted down. It was now about 5:00 PM Because of the last minute change in our beach landing area, we had become separated from our company but were able to join the rest of our company by nightfall. The day finally ended, and I was happy to still be alive.

Over the next few days, we moved inland in what seemed like a constant march interrupted by periodic firefights. On June 8 about twenty soldiers in another battalion of our regiment were either killed or wounded by friendly fire from British planes. We captured the town of Isigny-sur-Mer on the morning of June 9 and by noon were marching again, this time toward Saint-Lô. After marching another ten miles, we reached the German front lines and were forced to stop due to a lack of artillery support. We set up perimeter security on a hillside just beyond the village of Moon-sur-Elle.

Now both sides began probing each other's defenses. One night about 3:00 AM, a German patrol came down the road at our end of the secure area. Our men spotted them before they could do any damage. There was a brief firefight, but no casualties on either side. The Germans initiated several other probing attacks that night at other areas on our perimeter.

My partner and I were lying in foxholes in the middle of a field. Things were too quiet, so we decided to create some noise. I fired my automatic weapon into the night. That was not a smart move! The muzzle flash from my gun revealed our exact location, and we immediately received heavy return fire with tracer bullets flying all around us. Obviously, I did not try that again.

Early on the morning of June 12, we received orders to make contact with the 115th Infantry Regiment somewhere on our left flank. This was not unusual since, like the Germans, we were constantly probing enemy lines with patrols. This particular request was a little different though, since we knew the Germans were very close because of the skirmishes the night before. Our squad leader, John Spurr, selected five others to join him in this patrol—a point man, me, and three others. A full squad consists of twelve men.

We started out about 6:00 AM on a beautiful day and knew only that the friendly troops of the 115th Regiment were to our left. We did not know their exact location or the location of the enemy. With the point man leading the way, we moved straight ahead for two hedgerows then made a right turn through a gate and into a field. This was a bad choice. Just after I moved through the gate, a German machine gun opened up on us. The first rounds killed our point man. John and I dove into a trench, and the other three, who had not yet passed through the gate, retreated back to our lines.

As John and I inched forward on our stomachs, the machine gun kept firing. At that point John told me to turn around. This was hard to do without being hit, but the two of us crawled back to the gate. I tried desperately to dislodge the gate from its hinge so that we could make a run for it, but then John was hit by machine gun fire and seriously wounded. As we tried to figure out what to do, two German soldiers came up behind us and ordered us to get up. We complied.

John was in serious condition. I tried to help him, but my five-foot-seven frame was ill suited to carry John who stood at six four. We were led back to a place where some German soldiers were huddled in a machine gun nest. These were probably the same ones who were trying to kill us a few minutes before. John and I stayed there a short time before we were led to a company headquarters area. There I was interrogated by the company commander, a German captain originally from New Jersey, who spoke fluent English and knew more about my outfit than I did.

During the interrogation, I asked the captain if he could get a cart for John. He obliged, and we were taken to another area. John was still not doing well, but at least he was riding in a horse-drawn cart. After reaching the third area, John and I were separated. I later learned that he died on June 29, 1944, in a German military hospital in Rennes, France. Today his final resting place is on a hill in his hometown of Plymouth, Massachusetts.

The Germans marched me to a watchtower and forced me to climb a ladder to the top of it. I did so somewhat tentatively since I didn't know what was ahead. I barely made it to the top and then, exhausted, dropped to the floor. I must have slept for fourteen hours. A guard was stationed at the bottom of the tower, but he didn't have to worry about me escaping. June 12 was finally over—the end of a perilous day and the beginning of my eleven-month struggle for survival as a prisoner of war.

Looking Back

Janet Arthur

The beautiful Japanese red maple tree that I loved is dying. It stands in front of the only house my husband John and I owned for more than forty years. The house is in Canton; it was painted Carolina Dove Gray. The red tree could be seen through the large bow window at the front of the house. I would watch this tree changing colors. It was a deep crimson red in the spring. Then in the fall it would turn greenish. During the summer, I would water it whenever I was watering my flowers, especially in the dry years.

When the leaves had fallen on the ground around the tree in autumn, I would leave them in place as long as possible, so that nourishment from the leaves would go back into the tree. Also I thought there was a certain beauty in seeing the pretty colored leaves forming a perfect circle on the grass all around the tree.

Sometimes it snowed lightly over all the grass and entwining leaves—so beautiful. Every year the circles grew larger as the tree itself grew and flourished. When the tree was very young, visiting children were not allowed to climb it. Tender branches might break. John had planted this tree as well as every other tree and bush on the property except for one large Douglas fir tree at the back left corner of the land. Every tree and plant that John planted lived as long as we lived in the updated and thoroughly remodeled split-level house on Four Harrison Road.

Now this beloved tree is dead and has been cut down. We have only been away four years. It is difficult to say good-bye to an old friend.

“It’s Only for One Year”

Thomas O’Connor

For as long as I can recall, I have always enjoyed reading. As a youngster, I sought out all kinds of books about history at our local branch library, and I thought it would be fun to become a schoolteacher when I got older.

After graduating from the Boston Latin School in 1942, I completed my freshman year at Boston College before I went into the U.S. Army for three years, and then returned to the Heights to finish my undergraduate program in 1949. With the marvelous advantages of the G.I. Bill of Rights, I found that I could not only afford to go on for a master’s degree in history, but I could also enroll in a doctoral program. This would open up the possibility of teaching at the college level—something I had never dreamed of.

The practical realities of getting a college appointment at that time, however, were very dim, and I was forced to think of other employment possibilities. I began making applications for a position at the Boston Public Library. During my last two years at Latin School, I had a job shelving books at the BPL in Copley Square, and during my college years, I worked as an assistant in the Statistical Department. Prospects in this field looked fairly promising, as I made out application papers late in the summer of 1950. The school year was about to begin anyway, and there were obviously no teaching prospects in the near future.

One Thursday evening in early October, the telephone rang in my home. I picked up the receiver. It was the chairman of the history department at Boston College, Father James L. Burke, a Jesuit with a PhD from Harvard, a specialist in American constitutional history and a mentor as I completed my master’s work. “Mr. O’Connor,” he said in his deep rumbling voice, “would you like to teach at Boston College?” My head spinning in disbelief, I answered as soon as I could,

"Yes, Father." Then I added, "Definitely!" "Alright then, see me tomorrow morning in my office at ten o'clock." he replied, and the line went dead.

The next day I walked into the chairman's office where Father Burke was sitting at his desk. After a brief exchange of pleasantries, he explained that one of his instructors had suddenly left to take a higher-paying teaching position at one of the Boston public schools. There were four, fifty-minute courses in world history without an instructor. The classes had already started, the students were in place, and the textbooks had arrived. He needed someone in place for the first class at nine o'clock Monday morning.

"Would you like to teach, Mr. O'Connor?" he asked again. I immediately responded, "Yes." "Good," he replied, obviously relieved, and handed me a small piece of paper on which he had written down the amount of my nine-month salary—$2,650. In those days there were no fixed salaries. Since most of the teachers were Jesuits, deans or chairmen dealt with lay instructors on an individual basis. At that point, I didn't care how much it was, I would have taken this chance to teach at any price. I put the piece of paper into my pocket and said "That's fine, Father." "Thank you, Mister O'Connor," he answered. "We'll see you Monday morning."

I got up from my chair, walked over to the door, and had just put my hand on the doorknob when I heard his voice behind me. "Oh, Mr. O'Connor," he said, "just one more thing." I turned to face him, my hand still on the doorknob. "What's that, Father?" I asked. "Remember now," he announced, "this appointment is for one year only." "Yes, Father," I replied, opened the door, stepped outside, and stopped still for a moment to take it all in. Then, half aloud and half to myself, I heard myself saying: "One year, my foot! You are never getting rid of me." This was my big chance, and I was determined to make the best of it.

Early Monday morning, I made my way to Chestnut Hill with all kinds of questions swirling around in my mind. I had never taught a class before in my life. I had never given a lecture, nor had I ever organized a course curriculum. I was also aware that most of the students would be World War II veterans, as old as I was, and many of them much older. Taking a deep breath, I walked into the large wooden army barracks that was being used as a temporary classroom until a permanent building could be constructed. There were about sixty students sitting at their desk-chairs, surprised looks on their faces when they saw a brand-new instructor. I took my place at the rostrum and, in my best drill-instructor voice, announced who I was, took the required attendance, told them to open their books, and launched into my first college lecture.

That day literally flew by; it was exhilarating; it was everything I could have hoped for. I discovered that this was what I wanted to do for the rest of my life. And I did. I had the pleasure of serving as a professor of American history at Boston College for the next fifty years. And every now and then my wife, Mary, will tap me on the shoulder and say: "Remember, Tom, this is for one year only."

(Top L to R) John and Janet Arthur and Tom O'Connor
(Seated) Frank McDermott and Patricia and Paul Decot

How to Celebrate an Anniversary

Jennie Terminiello

How would you choose to celebrate your country's 200th birthday? To be more exact, the 200th anniversary of the signing of the Declaration of Independence. This was the dilemma facing my first grade classroom in 1976. I wanted to involve all the children, all twenty-seven of them, in the planning and the execution of what we decided to do.

How to fairly involve the brightest, the quickest, the not so quick, the easily challenged, the timid, the brave, the hesitant, and the unsure. The unsure—that included the teacher. Even though I was a mature age, I was the newest of the first grade teachers. This was going to be a challenge for everyone in this particular classroom.

We needed to talk about the significance of the Declaration of Independence. We had to find out about the first official flag of the United States.

We formed a circle and brainstormed. The suggestions were flying around, preceded by "and then we could." Some wanted to paint a mural or produce a play about how Betsy Ross designed the first flag. They liked the story that I had read to them, but the pictures inspired them even more. It set the mood for my suggestion that we make a Betsy Ross flag.

I thought we could all learn to use a punch needle. We practiced using embroidery hoops, burlap, and yarn. The children loved the idea that you could punch through the holes in the burlap and have a loop form on the opposite side without too much effort.

When we were through practicing, we were ready to consider the main project. We wanted something large and impressive. I asked my husband to make us a large frame for the very rustic burlap. We stapled the burlap tightly to the frame. I drew the flag on the reverse side of the burlap and now, we were ready to go. Not so fast—we needed a chart for scheduling the children as to who would be using the punch needle. We were almost ready. We needed something to make it more visually authentic. We (I) dug up a Martha Washington–type dress and paired it with a homemade dust cap for the girls. The boys could wear an extra large man's jacket with belt and a purchased tri-cornered hat. At last, the children worked on the flag and there were no problems about scheduling. We went alphabetically, and there was always one boy and one girl at the frame.

Of the possible disasters, there was just one. One of the children (I refuse to tell which one) found a loose piece of yarn and thought he or she could fix it by pulling. We lost a whole day's labor, but we chalked it up to enthusiasm and the desire for perfection.

The art teacher was so impressed by our efforts that she offered to frame our flag. She used large two-inch dowels and attached one to the top and one to the bottom of the flag. She braided some thick rope to the top so that we could hang it in our room for all to see. The assistant superintendent asked if he could hang the flag in his office. We took a vote, and it was unanimous the flag was going to hang in our classroom.

Becoming a Teacher

Anne Coghlan

My mother, Alice Blake Coghlan, was an important influence in the development of my formal education. She had been a teacher herself but urged me to explore the things that interested me. When I was very young and driving into Boston with her, we would pass a building with a green roof. She said, "That is where you will go to college." She had taken courses there herself and had been impressed with the teachers. She also knew that the founder had left money for the education of women to help them to be able to have a profession. Early on, the only thing I could remember was the green roof, and I told all my little friends that is where I would be going. The green roof was Simmons College.

I entered the Milton school system, starting with the Belcher School, an old wooden school around the corner from my house, for grades one through six. For grades seven through nine, I attended the Mary A. Cunningham Junior High School, which had just been built. In going from the seventh to the eighth grade, our class was sectioned as to level of accomplishment. I was placed in Miss Ella Smith's classroom. I noted that none of my friends were in this section. It was also evident to me that I was in a group who had deficiencies in at least reading and writing. I was often assigned to help other students. I, of course, told my mother, and she went immediately to see Miss Smith, who agreed I was in the wrong section. I had been overlooked because I was very quiet. This was the first time sectioning of students had been tried. My very short time in the first section of the eighth grade was a lesson for me.

World War II broke out in the early fall of my high school sophomore year, and a number of boys left for the armed services in our senior year. Those who survived were given their high school diplomas at the end of the war. Having taken the usual college preparatory courses, I applied and was accepted for admission to Simmons College.

In my freshman year at Simmons College, I majored in nursing. The night before I was to meet with my advisor to plan my courses for the next year, I told my mother I did not want to become a nurse. She said she knew that and asked what did I want to do. I indicated that I liked biology and the sciences, and that I would do that for the next three years—and I did. After graduation, I was hired as a technician on a project conducted by the Harvard Medical School at the old Boston City Hospital. I did not like the repetitive nature of laboratory work and the lack of contact with people. My mother asked me what I thought I might like to do. I said, teach biology, at least at the high school level.

I then went to the school of education at Boston University for two semesters of work for the M.Ed. After I completed all the course work, I got my first teaching position through B.U. It was to teach in the Science Department at Colby Junior College in New London, New Hampshire. I taught there for ten years, 1949 to 1959. I taught microbiology, three courses in chemistry, and histology.

I had one personal and professional experience at the end of my first semester at Colby related to my responsibility as a teacher. I remember this very vividly. I had just submitted my grades, and one student in microbiology had earned an F. I was called to the president's office and met with him and the dean. I was asked about the one student who had received a failing grade. I said I did work with her, but she constantly missed classes and failed all exams. I was aware of some family problems. It was pointed out to me that this was my first time teaching and grading. Then I was asked to change the grade so that she would pass. I thought for a few minutes. Then I said I was the person responsible for giving grades in my classes, had not made any errors, and would not change the grade! I left at that point. That night I called my mother, and she said, "You did the right thing."

During my ten years at Colby, I not only learned to keep up with my subject matter but also served on committees such as advising, alumnae, curriculum, and other faculty responsibilities. In my first year, I finished my dissertation at B.U. and received my M.Ed. Later I took off two semesters, took courses at the University of Vermont Medical School, and finished my dissertation for a master's in microbiology and immunology.

For nine summers at Colby, I worked for the Gordon Research Conferences. These conferences were established to allow scientists to meet—in groups of about 100—with others doing research in their fields. They met Monday through Friday mornings and Monday through Thursday evenings to give papers by specialists in their discipline. I attended all meetings because I ran the slides. Each week there were new topics such as Food & Nutrition, Cancer, Radioactivity, Corrosion, etc. Often the speakers were Nobel Prize winners. I learned a great deal even about corrosion.

I left Colby in 1959 because I had won a faculty fellowship from the National Science Foundation to finish a doctorate in microbiology. The Russians had launched Sputnik, and the United States found itself in great need of teachers with advanced degrees in the sciences.

I did my graduate work as a faculty fellow at the University of Minnesota for one year of classes and then went to the University of Rhode Island. After finishing, I went to Simmons where I sought a teaching position. To my delight, they were looking for a person with depth in microbiology and work in fungi and diseases, parasitology, and immunology. I was fully prepared for those areas.

The chairman in biology hired me on the spot. He had an NSF grant for the summer to teach microbiology to high school biology teachers. This was a common type of grant at this time. Experts sitting in their offices had developed lecture/laboratory outlines for these teachers. I was given an assistant who was a recent Simmons graduate in biology. She was bright and well trained.

The teachers we worked with were very interested in doing the laboratory experiments suggested. An interesting fact is that those who had developed the experiments forgot to remind these teachers about sterile techniques and problems with contamination. Several years later, I taught a similar course for three summers at the University of Rhode Island.

In the fall of 1963, I began my teaching of Simmons's students. I was glad to have had the experiences of graduate school between Colby and Simmons. The level of student achievement between the two schools was very different. Over time, I taught all the courses for which I had been prepared.

Simmons seniors had a requirement for working with faculty on some form of research, and I began this activity my first year.

I quickly fit into the mode of Simmons from my previous experiences. I was chosen my first year and through to retirement to be a faculty member on the Undergraduate Admissions Committee. This was hard work but great experience over the years. I did rotate on other committees. When I arrived, there was a college-wide activity to reexamine the undergraduate experience; it was called the Self Study. This took time, but I learned a great deal about all the teaching areas of the curriculum.

In the summer of my first year, I finished writing my Ph.D. thesis and received the degree. I had been appointed as an assistant professor and was immediately raised to associate professor with tenure. I was appointed professor on the regular timeline. In 1977, I was made dean of sciences for the undergraduate college. I was responsible for all the sciences, which included computers, psychology, health sciences of nursing and physical therapy, physical education and athletics. I remained professor of biology and dean of sciences until I retired. As dean, I elected to still teach at least one course and one laboratory section each semester. I felt that I should have direct student class contact since this was my administrative responsibility.

My position at Simmons kept me busy for a total of thirty-five years, seventeen as dean. In the latter, I met with a wide range of students. I found being a dean gave me a chance to be more helpful to all students. My plan had been to retire at sixty six years. I knew it was time for younger individuals to move upward. I had held a number of volunteer positions in Milton while I was working. These volunteer positions included chairman of the Milton Hospital, trustee of a lovely park in Milton, trustee of two schools, and member and chair of the Finance Committee. I retired to continue some of these positions through my retirement. The one thing I realized I missed the most from my teaching years was working with students. Several years after retirement, I moved to Fuller Village, an independent living community in Milton. This has been the right move from the beginning.

After retirement, and at the time of my sixtieth reunion, I received an honorary doctor of science degree. The very young woman who, while in her first semester of teaching and under pressure refused to change a failing grade, was named one of the Ten Best Teachers in connection with Simmons College's Century Celebration.

A Parade

Eleanor M. Reidy

Recently, when I was leafing through the pages of my book of life, my eyes rested on a page that showed me as a tiny little girl watching grown-up people hugging and kissing one another. There was such hilarity in the air and everyone was watching a parade.

I stood on the third step of my house, holding onto the doorknob so that I could see what everyone else was seeing. Old men in open touring cars were waving their caps. There was a flag standing in the back of the car and a fire engine, or maybe two or three fire engines following the touring cars.

The old men in the touring cars were Civil War soldiers. There was a marching band playing. I was in Savannah, Georgia, when it was a segregated city. The date was November 11, 1918. World War I was over! The war that was supposed to end all wars!

The Great New England Hurricane

Edith Yoffa

It had been windy and raining for several days before my parents picked me up at high school on September 21, 1938. We had planned to drive downtown in Norwich, Connecticut, the town where I lived, to buy a dress for Rosh Hashanah, the Jewish New Year. Downtown Norwich is on the Thames River, which runs up from New London that borders on the Atlantic Ocean.

While I was trying on a dress in the dress shop, we could hear sloshing noises under the floor. We wondered what was happening and questioned the salesgirl. "We have a lot of water in the basement," she explained, "because of the storm." She then opened the door to the basement, and in its semi-darkness we could see water moving partway up the stairs! We hurriedly made our purchase and left for home, realizing this was to be a dangerous storm. What we didn't know was that this would be a historic storm, New England's first hurricane since the 1800s.

There were no advanced warnings from the Weather Bureau. This storm had been developing into a hurricane over the past seventeen days, moving across the Atlantic Ocean and up the eastern coast of the United States. But meteorologists had not paid attention to its potential danger and did not alert the public.

My parents owned a hardware/housewares store on the west side of town, so my father left me off there to be with my older brother while he drove my mother home. I monitored the store while my brother worked feverishly in the basement lifting merchandise off the floor. I could see the river overflowing the loading dock that ran behind our store and neighboring businesses. Suddenly, the windows in the rear of the store facing the river started to break from the force of the wind and rain. I was terribly frightened and pleaded with my brother to come upstairs. He quickly did so, as the water had started to seep into the basement at a faster pace.

We covered the windows as best we could. Soon we heard a tremendous noise and could hear the water rushing into the basement. We carefully watched the stairway to the basement. The water kept rising, finally stopping one step below the floor level. We didn't know whether to stay or leave. We were terrified.

We went to the broken windows to investigate what was happening outside. There was the water, receding and taking much of our merchandise from the basement with it. We later learned that a tidal wave had moved up the coast, devastating Long Island, Providence, New London, and its beautiful beaches, and had continued up the river to Norwich.

Norwich is a hilly town. The only connection between the west side and downtown now was by rowboat. Our store entrance was just above the high water line. The wind had subsided, and the rain was light, so we could leave and walk home. We saw many uprooted trees along the way. Broken branches were everywhere. There was a tall twin pine tree in our backyard. When we arrived home, one tree had fallen across the road, and the other had fallen against the house, fortunately not causing much damage. But the town was devastated, and all electricity was lost.

Inspections by the Board of Health determined that the basement could be sanitized. Small merchandise that was salvageable could be taken to our home and sanitized in the two big washtubs we had in the kitchen. This took months to accomplish.

Several days after the storm, when the main roads were travelable, and having no electricity with the holidays coming up, we packed up the necessities—my new dress included—and drove to Bridgeport to my grandparents. Due to the damage from the storm through the towns along the way, the trip took several hours longer than usual. How grateful we were to be together, to have survived, and to not have suffered personal injuries.

The trauma had been great but The Great Hurricane of 1938 was past, and we now looked forward to a new year restored.

My Alaskan Adventure

Dorothy Gilman

It was sixty years ago that my husband, Hank, and I drove from Boston to Anchorage, Alaska, via the Al-Can Highway. We were newlyweds. Hank had just graduated from college and had signed a two-year contract with the Army Corps of Engineers. We pooled our meager resources, bought a new car for $2,200, and set off on our eight-thousand-mile grand adventure.

We drove from Boston to Great Falls, Montana, continuing to Edmonton, Alberta, Canada, and then onto the Al-Can Highway. In 1950, the Al-Can Highway that today is a four-lane highway was nothing more than a dirt road carved out of the wilderness. Hank had carefully planned where we would stop for gas, food, and lodging, as these necessities were often many miles apart, shabby, and uninviting. It would be a three-week trip!

When we arrived at Fort Richardson, the army installation in Anchorage, we were assigned to a barracks with nine other couples. Each of us had our own bedroom and shared a central area that housed bathrooms and showers. Privacy was non-existent! Our refrigerator was a milk crate that we placed outside our bedroom window in the below-freezing temperature.

Cars had head-bolt heaters that enabled us to plug into an electrical outlet on the outside of the barracks to prevent them from freezing. By arrangement, I had a placement in the steno pool and soon graduated to become secretary to Colonel Dorland, who looked very much like the famous movie star Van Johnson. He was a very kind man, and I really enjoyed working for him.

We adjusted very well to the Land of the Midnight Sun, so named because, in summer, daylight lasts for twenty-four hours. We enjoyed the long daylight hours. In winter, however, it is dark to dusk for twenty-four hours. Alaska is a beautiful state. Anchorage is surrounded by the magnificent Chugach Mountains. We walked on the amazing Matanuska Glacier and very carefully avoided falling into a crevasse so deep that we would disappear forever!

We met many wonderful people and had some fun times. In January, we celebrated a fur rendezvous. The men had to grow a beard or mustache or face the penalty of being locked up in jail for the night. We also had dog sled races that were enjoyed by all. But in 1951, there was not enough snow in Anchorage, so snow was shipped in from Fairbanks!

In August 1951, the time had come for us to return home. We spent seven enjoyable days on board the SS *Funston* on calm waters. The ship transported us, along with our car, to Seattle, Washington. From Seattle we drove down the West Coast to San Francisco, across the southern states, and then north, happy to be on our way home where we received a very warm welcome!

A Time When the Living Envied the Dead

Anna Gerut

As a survivor of the Shoah, I feel an obligation to leave a document of this tragic time in Jewish history. Every survivor went through a tragedy. This is my story.

I was born in Lodz, Poland. We were a family of eight. My parents were very well educated. My father was a scholar with two rabbinical degrees, but he was also a businessman. My mother strongly spoke and wrote in Polish, German, and Russian. Our lives were based on religion, education, honesty, and generosity. These values were ones we had to obey. We did not expect that any change could come into our lives, but the minute the Germans marched into Lodz in September 1939, everything changed.

All the Jewish people had to move to one small place called the Litzmanstadt ghetto. This was the first *gehenem* (hell). Here the hunger was so great that people died every day of starvation. The rations of food were so small that people were keeping their dead at home for a few days in order to get an extra piece of bread. Nothing seemed important, only where to find something to eat. Strong people pushed themselves to grab food wherever they could. Our family was a rabbinical one and could not behave this way. Instead we thought that a miracle would come to help us. We couldn't believe that the world would let us die of hunger. Yet, there were dead people in the streets all the time. They were taken away to the cemetery by horse and wagon.

As if this were not enough, the Nazis constantly conducted *aussedlungs* where people were taken away to the gas chambers. I remember saying that this was the time when the living envy the dead. "They don't have to suffer from cold and hunger any more."

Everyone looked for work. There were some German factories. My younger sister, Esther, found a job where she braided straw with her tiny hands to make shoes for the Germans. She would come home with swollen fingers. My brother, Moshe, pulled a wagon with cement somewhere, while my brother Emmanuel was too sick to work. I found a job in a corset factory and became a supervisor. We worked very hard with little food, and I came down with many illnesses but never stopped working. At night I found work in a kitchen so that I could bring home a bit of potato skin to make into a soup for the family. When I grew too weak to work both jobs, my mother took over the kitchen work.

Our mother cooked for the family with very little food. There was never enough, and we all began to look like skeletons. Mother used to promise us that after the war, she would cook up a big pot of potatoes and meat, and we all dreamed about it, but it never happened. In 1942, my father, Rabbi Nechemiah Warszawski, a tall, educated, handsome man, died of starvation at the age of forty-eight. His dear friend and colleague, Itchimueyer Levin, survived and became a cabinet minister in Israel. Who knows what sort of contribution my father could have made to the world had he survived.

In August of 1942 while my sister and I were out looking for food, there was a very big *aussedlung,* and my whole family was taken away forever. Let me take a moment to recall them: My mother Reyzele Warszawski, delicate and intelligent, age forty-four; my brother Emanuel, sensitive and bright, age eighteen; my brother Moshe, handsome and a good student, age sixteen; my brother Shlamek, a sweet boy, age nine; and my sister Noemi, the sweetheart of the house, age six.

It is very hard for me to return to these tragic days of my life. Why did such beautiful people have to be put to death? Hitler, *Imoch-shemoy*, had to get rid of all the Jews. This inhuman hatred cannot be forgiven. And this pain in my heart will never go away.

My sister Esther Bruche and I were the only survivors. She passed away in the United States at the age of fifty-four. In 1944, the ghetto was liquidated, and we were sent to Auschwitz, the next hell. Mengele the murderer was sending most of the people to the gas chambers. From the rest of us, they took away everything. We had to stand nude while Nazi soldiers shaved all our hair from top to bottom. They tried to make us feel inhuman, but they were the inhuman ones.

We received a piece of clothing with a red stripe of paint on the back. We were stuffed into barracks where we slept on the bare ground, one on top of the other like sardines. At 3:00 AM, we had to bring in garbage cans that contained the mud called coffee. After that we had to go out and stand barefoot in the mud for hours while the Nazis counted all of us. Back in the barracks, we were given a little soup and a tiny piece of bread. This was all we received until the next day when it all began again.

We were allowed to go to the toilet only once a day when they chose to take us. At the head of this place was a Nazi woman named Grasy who was a monster in a human body. Her job was only to beat us up. To survive one day was a miracle.

I used to think that perhaps I had died and gone to hell, but I didn't know what awful thing I possibly could have done to end up there. I was young and, although I didn't see any birds or flowers, I myself longed to become a bird and fly away. I would tell the world what was going on so that they could help us. But I now know they knew but were silent.

I dreamed of building an underground escape route, but they counted us continuously. We were never sure what day it was, but one day they said it was Yom Kippur, and I sang "Kol Nidre." Who knows, perhaps I lived in order to tell the story. But I am the only survivor of the entire family Warszawski. There were at least one hundred relatives. And of my mother's family, I have one remaining cousin: Lola Faivish of Toronto, Canada.

I must take a moment to recall my grandfather, Henoch Warszawski. He lived with his very large family in a little town near Warsaw called Jeziorna. He owned a great deal of land and property. On his property, he donated and supported a house of prayer and a cheder. I used to go to Jeziorna for summer vacations. It was a very happy place, filled with aunts, uncles, and cousins. My grandfather was well-known for his generosity. He was the town representative and was a major contributor to the Gere Rebbe's congregation.

When my grandfather was very ill, the rabbi from Ger, Rabbi Alter, came to Jeziorna to visit him. My grandfather died just before World War II. He was taken for burial to Ger so that the Gere Rabbe and his followers could attend the funeral. All the stores were closed, and there was a write-up in the newspaper about him.

From the Warsaw ghetto, the entire family Warszawski was taken to Treblinka. Included were my father's sister and her husband, Moshe Appelbaum, the editor of the Jewish newspaper, *Der Moment*, and their three children; such beautiful, noble people—what a great loss. I remember on Passover when my father used to tell us the story of the Jewish enslavement in Egypt, I never could have believed that I would become one of the tragic persons of Jewish history.

This tragic period of our history must be told from generation to generation like the reading of the Megillah on Purim and the Haggadah on Pesach. We must never forget what happened during the Shoah—and this must never happen again.

We lost our dearest six million Kidoshim. We have our country Israel. We must remember to support her. Our fathers prayed each day with the words "Shema Yisrael," and we must say "Am Yisrael Chai!"

The Proposition That Wasn't

Clara Martinelli

Like most golfers, my husband, John, was obsessed with the game. His famous words were, "I'm going up for nine." But his nine holes took all day. This annoyed and upset me, but, being a good wife, I didn't say anything—well, maybe a just little!

After giving this some thought, I decided I would learn how to hit that little white ball around the golf course. I signed up for some lessons. This would give me the opportunity to share the sport with John and be with him more often. Many wives would probably question this desire.

The pro was from Ponkapoag Golf Course in Canton where John played. My plan was to keep it a secret, and I looked forward to the day when I would be able to say, "Let's go up for nine." This worked well until the afternoon that John spotted me in the pro shop. Surprised he was not—he said it wasn't unusual to find me where there was clothing. Such was my reputation.

At the end of my fifth lesson, the pro informed me that "Next week we will go into the wood." Well, I certainly could not understand this. I was puzzled. After all, I did not hit a great shot from the fairway. Why would he think I would be able to hit a good ball from the woods?

This concerned me all week long. My thoughts were running away from me. What did he have in mind? I certainly did not say anything to John. I had never done anything to encourage this man. I must say he was handsome, but my John was just as good-looking.

After a couple of weeks, I finally worked up the nerve to speak to John about this situation. I asked him why he thought the pro wanted to take me into the woods. Needless to say, John had a great laugh for himself and then explained that these words meant that the pro was taking me to the next level: how to use the wooden clubs.

I not only felt foolish but relieved! This was the end of my great expectations of going "into the woods." I didn't turn out to be a Nancy Lopez pro, but I was good enough to say to John, "Let's go up for nine" and enjoy playing the game.

(Top L to R) Jack and Nancy Kearns
Jane and John Dooley
(Seated) Kurt Ladner, Nancy Souther, and Clara Martinelli

Honest to a Fault

Michael W. Ryan

On July 24, 1963, at the ripe old age of twenty-six, I was sworn in as a United States Postal Inspector, handed my credentials and government-issue brown leather briefcase, and ushered aboard a train that carried me to our nation's capitol and four weeks of intensive training in the various duties of a postal inspector. A major element of that training was devoted to the conduct of financial audits because, back then, inspectors audited every post office annually. With eight years postal experience under my belt at the time of my swearing in, and because much of that experience was on the financial side of the house, I had little difficulty absorbing the audit portion of my basic training. Still, our instructors emphasized the various ways in which a postmaster or finance clerk might embezzle postal funds, and that aspect of my training definitely captured my attention.

Phase II of the postal inspector basic training program consisted of four months of on-the-job work under the alternate tutelage of three or four seasoned inspectors. I was fortunate to have as my first instructor a highly regarded inspector, who, at that time, was still a bachelor. Roy, my instructor, wore Kuppenheimer suits and drove a top-of-the-line Chrysler sedan. As he had only a few post office audits to be done in his central Ohio territory when I arrived, we left his area before the first week had ended and drove to the heart of Appalachia: Hazard, Kentucky. Hazard was Roy's first duty station a few years earlier, and it was soon to become my first duty station, although I didn't know it at the time.

After a few days of uneventful audits, we left our motel one early fall morning and drove to a fourth-class post office (the smallest class of all) located up a backwoods hollow that was only accessible via an unimproved dirt road. In those years, many fourth-class post offices were located in postmasters' homes. This one was a cut above that, however, being located within a small, ramshackle, meagerly stocked general store.

The road ended at the general store, and Roy brought the car to a stop about fifty feet away facing the store; we observed a woman on the covered porch leaning against a canopy support and no doubt wondering who we were. Given our mode of transportation (a shiny new Chrysler) and dress (suits and ties), I imagine she took us for salesmen out to sell her something she didn't need and couldn't afford. Upon exiting the car, we walked back to the trunk from which we removed our government-issue briefcases, adding machine, and typewriter. Upon closing the trunk and reappearing in full view of the woman, this time with the tools of our trade in hand, she immediately stood erect, turned away from us and ran inside the store, closing the door behind her.

Keying on her obvious panic, Roy said, "Lets go" and immediately broke into a run with me close behind. We ran onto the porch and opened the door just as the postmaster turned away from the cash box, purse in hand, and placed her purse on a counter behind her. We then identified ourselves to her and informed her we were there to perform an audit. Roy chose not to question the postmaster's highly suspicious conduct at that time, and we proceeded with the audit that, in a fourth-class office, could be completed in as little as two to three hours. As the trainee, I performed the audit after Roy made it clear to me that I was not to inform the postmaster of the results.

In this type of audit, it's necessary to count each and every postage stamp, postcard, stamped envelope, and all of the money, right down to the very last penny. I did that with the expectation that, in this case, there would be no shortage; both Roy and I were satisfied the postmaster had placed a sum of money into the cash box between the time she ran into the store and the time it took us to reach the store. We assumed she had taken a sum of money from her cash box sometime prior to the date of our arrival and had only replaced the money that morning.

When I finished tallying her cash and accountable paper (stamps, etc.), I determined she was exactly $5.00 over what the cash box should have contained. Without saying anything, I showed my work papers to Roy. He looked at the figures, raised an eyebrow, and then turned his attention to the postmaster. Not one to beat around the bush, Roy said to her, “When we arrived, and you realized who we were, you ran into the office, took some money out of your purse, and put it in the cash box.” The postmaster, head bowed in submission, replied, “Yes, sir, I did.” Roy then asked, “How much money did you put in the cash box?” and she replied, “Five dollars.” Probing further, Roy asked, “Why did you do that?” The postmaster responded simply, “I didn’t want to get caught short.”

As it turned out, this was the first audit this relatively new postmaster had undergone, and she had heard stories from older postmasters about how difficult, overbearing, and mean postal inspectors can be when they discover a shortage. Roy proceeded to give her a stern lecture about the importance of not mixing personal funds with postal funds. He then allowed her to remove the $5.00 but warned her that any future overage would be considered post office money and would be accounted for as an unexplained overage that would be remitted as postal funds.

The lesson I gleaned from this memorable event was simple. It reminded me of what my years of postal employment had already taught me: the vast majority of all postal employees are honest to a fault.

In Flanders Fields

Francine Weistrop

There are very few among us who did not read, hear, or possibly memorize the poem, "In Flanders Fields" by John McCrae, a tribute to those young American soldiers who fell in battle during World War I. But once past high school, I did not give it much more thought except for every Armistice Day, when I read it to my classes and talked about the meaning of serving one's country.

When our children were old enough to go to camp, my husband, Rabbi Jerome Weistrop, and I decided we would take overseas vacations by ourselves. We were active travelers, visiting many countries on several continents. As usual, we made sure to see the tourist highlights: the Eiffel Tower, the Duomo in Florence, the canals of Venice, the peaceful countryside in England, the Western Wall in Jerusalem, etc. As most tourists, we took many photos; in those days they were slides. We eagerly showed them to all who were willing to look, and then we went on to plan the next trip and put all the sights of that summer in the recesses of our memories. They were lovely memories, but they did not speak to us in a personal language.

That all changed when we took a driving trip through France and Belgium. We stopped to admire the scenery, to purchase fruit from a little boy sitting at the roadside. We packed picnics with food purchased at farmers' markets, and tried to use our high school French. It was a pleasant but altogether unremarkable time, that is, until we saw the sign: AMERICAN MILITARY CEMETERY, FLANDERS FIELDS. How could we pass it by? Both of us had learned that poem in our public school classes in New York City. It was written about the same time our parents arrived at the shores of this country, and it gave us an identity. We were American children; those soldiers were our countrymen. We turned off the main road and drove to Flanders Fields.

As we gazed at the scene before us, a line from the poem came to mind, “between the crosses, row on row.” And indeed there were rows and rows of simple white crosses. We stopped to read the names and the dates. It did not take long to realize most of those buried there had died at the ages of eighteen or nineteen. It also did not take long to realize that most of them had never married and had no living family to honor them or to visit their graves. We knew what we wanted to do. It was not possible to stop at all of the graves, but we stopped at as many as we could and read each name aloud.

And then we noticed something unexpected. Every so often, between those crosses, was a white Star of David indicating here was a soldier of the Jewish faith. These young people also never lived long enough to have children, and their families were also not alive to visit their graves, to say the Jewish mourners’ prayer. This had to be our responsibility. We owed it to them as we owed reading aloud the names of the other soldiers who lay under those white crosses.

So we walked from star to star. Jerome put on his yarmulke (skull cap) and said the prayer at each of the starred graves in our vicinity. We knew those parents whose sons never returned would have wanted it done, and we did it for them. But we also did it for ourselves.

Memories of My Wartime Childhood

Blossom Glassman

There are days that begin like all the others before them—bright with promise and the comfort of the usual routines of daily life. Sunday December 7, 1941, was just that kind of day. I am six years old.

My sister Elaine and I warm ourselves in the kitchen and set about to play "store." Suddenly, the music from the radio stops, and the solemn, stern voice of President Roosevelt rises in volume. "Today, the Japanese bombed Pearl Harbor. This is a day that will live in infamy. America is at war!" And I am suddenly very frightened, not quite understanding what this all means.

"Will they bomb us next?" I asked my sister Elaine who is twelve. "Of course not!" she answers with authority. Relieved, I happily return to the security of my childhood cocoon. But on that wintry day, the world and my life would change dramatically for the next four years.

Almost immediately, the war effort is on. The call to service is electric. "Uncle Sam Wants You!" posters pop up everywhere. Young men in our neighborhood, family, and friends, leave for far-off countries to fight the enemy: the German, Italian, and Japanese armies of Hitler, Mussolini, and Hirohito. We say our good-byes with tears and long hugs, and I wonder if they will ever return. I hold my dad's hand tightly, grateful that he is over the age for the draft.

Uncle Sam Needs Everyone! And on the home front I am enlisted to flatten our tin food cans that will be used for manufacturing airplanes and other war equipment. It's fun to stomp on each one until it flattens into a silvery pancake. I toss them into the storage barrels for the scrap metal drive pickup, and I wonder about all the planes and bullets we are helping to manufacture.

By 1942, rationing has become part of our life, and throughout the country, you can't go to the grocery store and buy as much of the foods on your shopping list as you want. You can't fill up your car with gasoline whenever you like. Every family has coupon books with stamps that allow them to buy only small amounts of meats and foodstuffs such as butter, sugar, and coffee. Rubber goods, shoes, clothing, and many other items are in short supply.

My mother misses her silk stockings, and I really miss my bubble gum! But our sacrifices at home mean that more of these items are going to our soldiers overseas where they are desperately needed. We are saving lives! And as my mother points out at almost every meal, "Finish your meal. Remember, children in Europe are starving!" Leaving anything on my plate fills me with unbearable guilt. If only I knew the addresses of those children in Europe, I would gladly send them all my fish and vegetables!

Life moves on and assumes a strange balance between dealing with the war day by day, with all its excitement and apprehension, and maintaining our usual life routines. Air-raid drill alarms interrupt the school day without notice. We are trained to line up and follow teachers to the school basement or, at other times, to crawl under our classroom desks until the drill is over. Sometimes we miss our arithmetic or penmanship lessons, (hurrah!) but nothing interferes with recess, when our restless children's spirits can burst onto the playground and find release in games of Red Rover, Dodge Ball, Jump Rope, and Rattlesnake!

At home in the evening, the blackout shades are drawn whenever the air-raid sirens are heard. Volunteer neighborhood wardens walk the streets to make sure that no house lights can be seen from the outside, just in case enemy bombers were flying overhead. My family and I sit in our darkened house. The radio croons its soft music, and the dimmed light casts almost Halloween-like shadows on the walls. It's cozy, exciting, and scary, and I'm relieved when the all clear is sounded. All fears are forgotten until the next time.

My oldest sister, Rhoda (now sixteen) and her friends are doing a great job for the war effort. They take turns arranging after school dance parties at their homes for the local soldiers stationed at Fort Devens. Whenever the date is set at our house, I fly home from school to find the living room alive with jitterbugging teenagers dancing with young soldiers who look so very handsome in their uniforms. The music of Glenn Miller,

Tommy Dorsey, The Andrews Sisters, and Benny Goodman fill the room. In the corner of the room, another soldier plays favorite tunes on our piano, and sometimes I'm invited to play "Chopsticks" with him. Others sing along, their voices rising in harmony. And although I'm only eight, I'm part of the crowd, joining right in, knowing all the lyrics, and dancing the jitterbug. I feel like a teenager myself! These are some of the best days of my young life!

But it is the news that I never quite get used to. My mom and dad are intent on listening to the war reports on the radio every night. The room is filled with the intense voices of Gabriel Heatter and Walter Winchell. I can see the concern on their faces, hear their whispered comments when I'm not in the room. Things must be going badly! When we go to the movies, it is there that the calamity of war becomes real for me. Every feature is preceded by Movietone News with movie film of raging battles in strange sounding places like Tarawa, Burma, Guadalcanal, Warsaw, and Normandy. Aircraft "dogfights" fill the screen, bombing raids destroy cities in an instant while voices of imbedded reporters provide eyewitness accounts of death and devastation. There is much footage of Hitler and his fierce goose-stepping army, faces half hidden under dark metal helmets. I see war refugees and so many children just like me, forced to live through this war. And then the images disappear, the main feature begins, and I happily watch and laugh at Abbott and Costello.

I was ten years old when the war ended in August 1945, after Germany had surrendered and Japan was forced to surrender after the destruction of Hiroshima and Nagasaki by the atom bombs. I was old enough to read the news accounts of human misery, the sufferings of civilians, adults, and children who had lived through those years; old enough to learn about the Holocaust and see actual footage of the hell that it was, and, later, to read the story of Anne Frank. And I would think over and over again of how fortunate it was for me that my grandparents had chosen to leave Russia and come to America long ago and provide a safe homeland for our family.

But for them, how very different a childhood mine would have been!

A Sunday to Remember

Elena MacIsaac

I was six years old when my brother was drafted into the U.S. Army. He spent the next several months at Camp Edwards on Cape Cod. I turned seven that summer when my brother spent his nickels to call home. Remember when phone calls were a nickel? His major complaint was missing my mother's home-cooked Italian meals.

So on a rainy Sunday afternoon, we all piled into my father's closed-panel truck with a bowl full of spaghetti and meatballs and headed for the cape. That day was Sunday, December 7, 1941, the day the Japanese attacked Pearl Harbor and the last time we saw my brother for six years!

My Parents' Courage in the Great Depression

Elaine Pinderhughes

The Great Depression left many people with memories of struggle, pain, deprivation, and loss—of jobs, wealth, resources, comfort, pleasures, and much more. Living in the nation's capital, I remember the panic that seemed to engulf everyone as headlines screamed about the panic on Wall Street, the suicides of financiers, and the long lines of people trying to save their funds before the escalating bank closings and lockout of customers.

There were also the bonus marchers, the veterans of World War I who came by the thousands from across the country to demand the bonus pay they had been promised. They camped out on the grounds of the Washington Monument and near the White House. I still have visions of them warming themselves over barrels of blazing firewood, appearing ragged, dirty, unshaven, and desperate. Eventually, order broke down, and the National Guard dispersed the veterans—with bullets as I recall.

My father, a dentist, had had a flourishing practice. But now in this grave crisis, he had practically no patients. A southern man, he had always insisted that my mother, who had worked before their marriage, remain at home as a housewife. So with no other income, they could pay neither the mortgage, the real estate taxes, nor the many bills that were swamping them.

Even I was aware of their shame that our names appeared in the daily newspaper on the list of delinquent taxpayers, and of their terror that they would lose everything. Mother warned me that one day when I came home from school there would probably be a FOR SALE sign on the house. So each day when I came back and rounded the corner just before our house, my heart would beat faster.

But that day never came. It never came because Mother rescued us: she saved us from ruin by securing a job in the government that would never have been hers had it been known that she was a Negro. Mother was so fair skinned that even Negroes thought she was white. Now my sister and I were dark-skinned like our father and were often stared at when with our mother or mistaken for someone else's children, not hers.

We were frequently reminded of this on our weekly Sunday afternoon drives; whenever our car approached a stoplight—and my sister and I just knew it would happen—first one and then all the passengers in the car adjacent to ours, would turn to stare at us. My sister and I, in self-defense, peering out of the back window as our car drove off, would make ugly faces at these staring souls and poke out our tongues. Of course, our parents never knew this was happening.

We also had friends who, along with their families, looked like mother and thus were able to "pass" going downtown to shops, theatres, and restaurants where, in our nation's capital, Negroes were, by law, not allowed. But mother had always insisted that she would never go anywhere her children could not. For three years, she kept this job, going into another world that we could not enter. Every day my father drove her to work, dropping her many blocks away from her place of employment so that no one would see her with him. One day I heard her on the phone laughing with a friend about the fact that the women in her office wanted to plan an outing together with their children. For me, being at a very formative age and eager to be like my beloved mother, this was anything but a joke.

In later years, I have reflected on what it must have meant to my parents for mother to have done this deed. How desperate must they have been that it became necessary for her to enter a world that regarded her people as inferior and undeserving? As an imposter, she could have been exposed in shame, surely arrested, and possibly subjected to much worse if the truth had been known. And my father who was such a proud man—what courage must he have summoned to manage his powerlessness to protect his wife as she went into that hostile other world, to endure this unspeakable insult to his pride and manhood?

Senior Indiscretion

Paul and Patricia Decot

Picture two senior citizens driving down Route 1 toward Portsmouth, New Hampshire on a dreary day in Ogunquit. Cruising along, Paul and I were reading political signs and came upon one bearing the same name as a contractor for whom Paul was currently designing kitchens. On our return trip from Portsmouth, we noticed another sign bearing that name, but this one was lying on the ground and in bad shape. Deciding it would be fun to put the sign on the contractor's lawn as a joke, we turned the car around and went back to pick it up; we were driving a bright red Grand Marquis. Paul pulled over and popped the trunk, whereupon I got out, picked up the sign, and deposited it the trunk.

Upon arriving back at our cottage, we received a phone call from our daughter at home in Boston; she was wondering if her father was playing a joke because she had just received a phone call from the York Police asking to speak with Mr. Paul Decot. To make a long story short, it was not a joke; someone had spotted our bright red Grand Marquis, taken our license plate number, and called it in to the York Police.

We called the police station and were instructed to come in with the sign. We arrived at the station, Paul carrying the sign with me following. The two officers behind the glass had a look of astonishment on their faces when they saw two gray heads carrying the sign. The officer we were to see was out on another call, so we were told to take a seat and wait. We did so and used the time to ponder our fate. We were scared to death.

When the investigating officer arrived, he brought us into his office where we related our story about thinking how much fun it would be to play a joke on our contractor friend. Luck was with us because the officer, realizing our advanced age, was convinced we were telling the truth. He did inform us, however, there was a $500 fine and possible arrest for removing political signs from the roadway. We were very naive and completely oblivious of this law.

The officer had already spoken with the candidate whose sign we had taken, and with the district attorney who wanted to prosecute us, smoothing things over and assuring them the sign was being returned. Exiting the police station, we were sure the two officers behind the glass were having a good laugh at our expense.

Returning to Littlefields Village, we related our escapade to some of our friends. Littlefields Village is much like Fuller Village in that word spreads like wildfire, and we became the butt of many jokes for the rest of that season.

Our senior indiscretion is a memory we will never forget, and one that will never be repeated.

A Love Story

Marjorie Seery

At the age of eighteen I fell in love with a "gorgeous pair of brown eyes." My wonderful parents were devastated. They were broken-hearted, and I for them because I loved them dearly. My Charlie, twenty-two years old, was already employed with a major company—his office was at the Statler Building in Boston.

There were sessions with my grandmother, godmother, aunts, etc., all trying to convince me I was "too young." My grandmother said, "You don't know what love is. It's just a word you don't really know the meaning of." We dated for six months, were engaged for three months, and then married in a small wedding in our church.

We moved into a downstairs apartment in a two-family house in Newton. One and a half years later, our daughter Joan was born, and two years later we were blessed with another daughter Carol. My parents' home was just walking distance from where we lived, and I would go to visit my mother. She would rock her little granddaughter in her rocking chair and sing to her and, later, with Carol—oh, how she loved them!

Charlie and I loved being young with our girls—running on the beach in the summer and coasting down a nearby hill in the winter. When I was eight years old, my grandmother gave me a piano, but I did not take it when I married. I did miss it! Then one Valentine's Day, the door-bell rang and a man said, "Your piano is here"—a brand-new Lester Spinet with a card on top: two words "Love, Charlie."

We had been saving to buy a house, and one day we drove to our favorite town, Needham, and purchased a nice piece of land. Three months later, we started building our dream house. Almost every evening after dinner we would drive to Needham to see what was accomplished that day, as wood, bricks, shingles, pipes, wires, etc., almost miraculously became a beautiful house.

The excitement, happiness, and love we all shared at that time I will never forget. A new life began when we settled into our new home; new grammar school for the girls, new neighbors, new friends, etc. Our daughters were wonderful growing up and keeping busy. Our home was filled with their friends and ours. There were some days with sickness or a minor problem here or there, but love always held us close.

On our fifteenth wedding anniversary, Charlie bought me a lovely Washington berry tree—a flowering tree—and planted it outside our window in the dining section of our kitchen. I loved it! That evening, we went to dinner—just the two of us. On the way home, we were passing a little side road where we often parked when we were dating to say our "good nights." Suddenly Charlie pulled over to the spot. Being overdramatic, he loosened his tie and reached over to hug me. A large flash of light was in my face and there stood a police officer. I could not stop laughing. "What so funny?" he asked. I told him we were married. "Hey, Joe, they say they're married." "Yeah," said Joe, "but not to each other." We finally convinced them.

Charlie loved parties, and we had many of them. Singing around the piano with family, friends, and neighbors was always fun. It was a home filled with fun and love.

Friends and neighbors of ours had horses, and both daughters learned to ride. Carol was more accomplished and passionate about the sport than Joan. Our land and our friend's land bordered the property of a business college that allowed the girls to ride their trails. When Carol was fourteen years old, she was in a very large horse show on the Holliston-Sherborn line. We watched with excitement and pride as Carol went through all the required paces, her blonde hair flying from under her riding cap. Then, three riders were chosen to move up for the judging; Carol was one of them. It was so quiet. Suddenly Carol's horse reared very high. I was not worried as I had seen this happen before, but I remember thinking that this may cost her the prize. Then her horse reared again and went over backward; horse and rider hit the ground simultaneously. The horse, with all fours up, rolled over—and over Carol—to regain his footing. I screamed, "Ambulance and police escort to Newton Wellesley Hospital!" to the doctors we knew.

I rode in the ambulance with Carol; Charlie and Joan rode behind us. Our doctor came out to the ambulance to meet us and started giving orders to the help around him. Charlie, Joan, and I huddled together waiting. Then we were told, "Your daughter is in critical condition. She is hemorrhaging internally and has a broken and crushed pelvic cradle. She needs two surgeons—one internal and one orthopedic." Charlie said, "Get the best." Only God's love and our own love enabled us to endure the surgeries. Carol was hospitalized for three months. I will never forget the family, friends, and neighbors who poured out their love to us. I went to the hospital every day and prayed to God that I would not hear Carol moaning in pain as I got off the elevator.

When Carol was finally recovering at home, I knew a new life would begin for me. I had to get a job. Even with Charlie's good income, the cost of her injuries was exorbitant. At first Charlie did not want me to work, but then gave me his love and blessings. We did not have insurance then. I went to work for a well-known company in their credit department. My work was accounts receivables. Four months later, my credit department manager called me to his office and told me the vice-president and executive director of advertising wanted to see me. I thought, "Oh, what did I do?"

I asked why he wanted to see me and was told the vice-president needed a new public relations person and wanted to interview me. At first I was reluctant to go but, when I learned how much more money it would be, I went out and got the job. A whole new world opened up for me. I found work that I loved. My work was very diversified. My favorite part was working with fashion editors from major newspapers in major cities across the country, national publicity. This offered me the opportunity to write—which I truly enjoyed—project after project, year after year. I retired at age sixty-two.

After high school, Joan and Carol went to a two-year Boston business school, Joan to become a medical secretary and Carol a legal secretary. Our girls married in the same year, Carol at age twenty in June and Joan at age twenty-two in October. They walked down the open staircase of our dream home before going off to a very large church wedding and reception. Oh, the love Charlie and I shared for our lovely daughters! Carol presented us with our first grandchild, a girl, then Joan also had a girl later that same year—the first two of eleven grandchildren. We were grandparents at age forty-two and forty-six. Our love for our grandchildren, as for our daughters, was profound and unconditional.

In 1951, Nat King Cole recorded a song entitled "Too Young"; the lyrics go like this:

They tried to tell us we're too young,
too young to really be in love.
They say that love's a word, a word we've only heard
but can't begin to know the meaning of.
And yet we're not too young to know
this love will last though years may go.
And then some day they may recall
we were not too young at all.

We could not believe the words, it was as if the song had been written for us—my grandmother's words of so long ago!

On my fiftieth birthday, Charlie took me to a jewelry shop in the Statler Building. He had a gift for me: a double gold chain bracelet with one charm: a heart with a rose on it, my favorite flower. Also, there was a ruby, my birthstone. Engraved on the back was, "We were not too young at all. Love, Charlie."

Charlie retired at age sixty-two after forty years with the company; that gave him seven years to enjoy playing golf at our club and completing many beautiful paintings, his two favorite hobbies. At age sixty-nine, the dreaded disease of Alzheimer's began. The doctor's diagnosis: "a nonclassic case." We stayed in our dream home through his seventieth birthday. Then we were forced to sell and move to one-floor living in a beautiful large condominium in Canton, to be near our daughter Joan and her husband. It was 1987 and our golden wedding anniversary. Our wonderful family gave us a huge celebration dinner dance at our club. Friends and relatives from all over the country were there. Earlier in the day, we went to the church where we were married and renewed our marriage vows.

Still in early stages of Alzheimer's, Charlie was able to dance with me to "Too Young" and enjoy dinner at the head table. Our oldest grandson gave a beautiful speech and toasted us. What a tribute it was! He said in part, "Our grandparents have taught all of the family the true meaning of love."

Charlie had three grand mal seizures, but his sweet loving personality never changed, "a nonclassic case." I had turned our den into a hospital room, complete with wheelchair, electric bed, etc. Every morning a nurse would come to attend to his bath, etc. In the afternoon, an aide would come to sit while I food-shopped and ran miscellaneous errands.

In the last two years of Charlie's life, he could not walk, talk, or feed himself, or even turn on his side in the bed. After the nurse had bathed him, she would bring him in his wheelchair to the kitchen where I would feed him his cereal. He always knew me even until the very end. When Charlie would come into the kitchen, so clean, his hair still dark and damp from the shampoo, I would bend over and kiss him, saying, "Look at you, you're so handsome, I love you." Charlie would look up at me with those "gorgeous brown eyes," as tears poured from them down over his face, telling me he loved me too! I felt his love to my core. Charlie died at home with family at age seventy-six in 1991.

As I write my love story, I am ninety-one with two daughters, eleven grandchildren, and thirty great-grandchildren. On my ninetieth birthday, my family gave me a beautiful luncheon birthday party at a restaurant on the water at New Seabury, Cape Cod. My best gift was, beginning with the youngest, who could read and write, my great-grandchildren standing before me and reading "Why I Love Nana." Their reasons were wonderful. The party ended with my daughters reading "Why I Love My Mother." The children also made a ninetieth birthday book for me containing all of their written works.

I treasure this gift. The love goes on!

(Top L to R) Virginia Coghlan, Elena and Joe MacIsaac
Jennie Terminiello
(Seated) Francine Weistrop, Paula Silbert, Eleanor Reidy

Near the Blue Hills

John Hemenway

I was brought up as the third generation on my grandfather's estate in the Canton/Milton area near the Blue Hills. My father inherited part of this land and later he gave me seven acres. In 1950, I built my own house for Phoebe, my wife, and later my four children.

I had returned in 1945 after three years in the army. I had attended and graduated from Harvard, Class of 1946. I had met Phoebe, a Radcliffe student, and started work in a brokerage house.

In 1953, my career suddenly changed. The director of the New England Forestry Foundation died, and I was offered his position as executive director. This was a conservation organization offering practical forest management for woodland owners throughout New England. At that time it was something new. The idea was to change from the usual destructive practices such as wanton "high-grading" in favor of careful cutting under the eye of a trained forester for healthier, more productive woodlands. I served there for about thirty years.

On the side, I purchased—parcel by parcel—my own spread of timberland in central Vermont in an area known as Taylor Valley. This investment of many acres now seems imposing, but, at that time, it was incredibly cheap. My first purchase of one thousand acres cost only $4.00 per acre.

In the 1960s, I served as tree warden in Milton. At that time, we had a small sawmill off Randolph Avenue. This utilized fallen street trees that were sawn to provide timbers and lumber for many town uses. What a shame this was later diverted to some other use. It was a successful means of reducing waste while providing useful products for the town.

About this time, with essential help from John Cronin, executive secretary of the Select Board, we established one of the early conservation commissions in Massachusetts and New England. One of several projects of particular interest today in 2010 was the construction of a substantial flood-control dam at the corner of Harland Street and Unquity Road. It involved substantial cost, although the cost was reduced 75 percent by state and federal conservation subsidies.

Just recently, with the heavy rains, this dam prevented extensive residential flooding. Indeed, had it not been for this project, many houses on Canton Avenue and in the Parkway area would have had flooded basements. Water was backed up and spread harmlessly over more than one hundred acres previously set aside in a conservation easement for this purpose. This was for a watershed of about eight square miles.

We are fortunate to live in a town that has planned ahead for these and other conservation needs.

The Lake

Sharon Becker La Bree

When I was a kid, my folks bought property near a lake. At the time, the roads around the lake were not yet paved. I remember telling my dad, as I messed up his hair, that the parts I made in his hair were like the roads at Lake Forest. It was in that lake that I learned to swim and to dive. Swimming came easy, but diving head first into that dark lake took me a while to accomplish. Once I learned, however, I became an avid diver off the raft and even did the envied backward dives.

We'd often go to the lake after supper on hot nights. One night, as we arrived, we overheard some young boys talking about us. One said, "Who are they?" The other replied, "It's the fat guy and the kid that jumps right in." Those words were a family joke for a long time. After that, though, Dad did go on a diet. But, I continued to "jump right in."

Dad soon bought a small rowboat and taught me to row and to fish. There were some pretty good-sized fish in the lake. I remember seeing trout, pickerel, perch, and bass. I was happy just catching sunnies. I remember one early morning when we were fishing out by the dam, I got a really strong bite. My line was being pulled down hard. Dad said, "I'll bet you have an eel on the end there." Being deathly afraid of snakes, I screamed,—as he began to reel in my line—"If you bring that thing into this boat, I'm jumping out." I guess he knew I was serious because he just laughed and cut the line. It was a while before I lived down threatening to jump in with the rest of the eels.

In the early days, I could go to the lake only if accompanied by my parents. As I got older, I was allowed to go alone. Mom would drop me off on summer after-noons as she returned to work after lunch, and pick me up on her way home after 5:00 PM. Those were wonderful afternoons. There was a whole gang of us kids who would swim and play in the water for hours. Of course, there was the draw of the boys. But most of all, it was just the fun of hanging out with other kids.

I took a Red Cross lifesaving course at the lake when I was sixteen and scored higher than any other kid, even better than the boys. I never did win the across-the-lake swim race, though. I didn't have the stamina to swim freestyle or "overhand," as Dad called it, the entire way across. I had to breaststroke, sidestroke, or float on my back a good bit, but I entered every year. It was the watermelon race where I shone. I remember diving into the water toward that greased melon, coming up under it, and pushing it ahead of me all the way to shore. No one could catch me. I'd get it in close to shore, stand up, pick up that slippery melon and stagger up to the judge. No one ever wanted to take it from me, so I'd end up holding it until I was awarded the trophy. Then I had to get it back into the water for the next group's try.

Even in the winter, the lake was a great place. It would freeze over entirely—except for the spot where the ducks swam—and was a wonderful place to ice-skate. That duck hole was the cause of one near tragedy. Two boys, friends of mine, were racing, and one fell and slid into the open water. Fortunately, the other boy was a quick thinker and got down on his belly, reached his hands to his friend and was able to pull him out. He took a chance, but turned out to be a hero.

I loved to ice-skate and was quite a good skater in my day. I'd rush home from eighth grade, change my clothes, grab my skates, and run to the lake. It was a good distance from where we lived. It took me about twenty minutes to get there, so I would have about and hour and a half to skate before Mom picked me up after work. Again, there was a boy involved, but it was all good fun.

I remember one Christmas Eve we were going to visit friends who lived on the lake, and I was in a rush to leave and meet my friends for skating. I was being the typical teen, encouraging my parents to hurry up. When Dad—who had gotten Mom a new ring for Christmas and was planning to surprise her with it at the get-together—said to me, "Cool it, young lady, it's not just your Christmas Eve. It's our Christmas Eve, too." I think that was the first time I realized my parents had hormones, too.

Indoor activities also flourished at the lake's clubhouse. I learned to ballroom dance at the dance classes for preteens.

Then, I attended most of the teen dances as I got older. I learned to tie flies with the fishing group, and then to fly-fish with them. I bowled with the duckpin group and held a fairly good average for a girl.

Some of the most memorable events in my life occurred at the lake: my first kiss, my parents' twenty-fifth wedding anniversary party, and my bridal shower are among them. It's a place I haven't seen in a long time, but it's a place I'll never forget.

Meeting General Eisenhower

Hy Rossen

I graduated from the Massachusetts College of Optometry in 1943—at the height of World War II. I immediately joined the army. I didn't have a license; I hadn't even taken the licensing exam. I had no experience; I was just straight out of college. I got into a medic outfit that had very rigorous training. The training was the same as the infantry, crawling through mud and everything.

In December of that year, 1943, I was shipped over to England for further training. They were getting ready for the invasion of France. It was very rough training. One day when we were in this training session, the commander of the session said he had an order for three men at SHAEF, Supreme Headquarters Allied Expeditionary Force, General Eisenhower's Headquarters.

We were told to grab our clothes (we trained in overalls), and the next day we went by truck to London. We walked into the most gorgeous, magnificent building. From mud to this handsome building! We got nice clothes, a nice place to live—believe me, a far cry from where we lived when we were in the infantry. I loved the job; we were handling secret documents. It was the time of planning for D-Day.

One day I was given the choice of staying in the adjutant general's office or going to the eye clinic. I elected to go to the eye clinic. There were three optometrists in one building, and our job was to take care of the headquarters people for all illnesses except if it was serious enough, we would ship them to a medical facility.

A couple of days after the invasion, I got a call in the evening; they came to the hut where we lived. "Rossen, report to General Eisenhower's office tomorrow morning first thing." I did and was greeted by his secretary, Kay Summersby. She asked, "Who are you?" I told her, and she told me the general had broken his glasses in the invasion.

I didn't have a Jeep, so I took the bus into London. They had an area there where they made G.I. glasses for soldiers. I explained I had a pair of civilian glasses, and the head guy yells, "We don't repair civilian glasses!" So I told him they were General Eisenhower's, and he of course repaired them.

A short time later, the whole headquarters moved to Normandy and, shortly after that, to Versailles. One day, my captain said, "Rossen, General Eisenhower is coming in to have his eyes examined." My captain was an eye, ear, nose and throat specialist, and I figured he was going to examine Eisenhower, but he informed me I was to do it. Eisenhower came in with a couple of aides, two or three officers. I examined Eisenhower myself. His examination was routine, there was nothing wrong with his eyes. But apparently in the chaos of the D-Day invasion, his glasses were broken. I arranged a super-fast repair, as noted above!

I had gone to Europe on the *Ile de France*, a troop ship the government got from France. It was a great big ship and could go faster than the submarines. The weather was good—nothing to it. It was March of 1946 when I was ready to come home, and some of the other guys were going to wait until summer to travel. I found out why when I boarded the ship and smelled oil. It took fourteen days to cross the Atlantic compared to the four days it took going over. Everybody on the ship was sick.

They took us to Fort Devens and gave us a great meal and our discharge papers. Then they put us on a bus to Boston where I took a cab ride home to Mattapan. It was quite an experience for someone who had never been out of Massachusetts until he joined the army!

My Wonderful Life as an Air Force Wife

Janet "Jan" Tobin

I was born in Dorchester, Massachusetts, St. Mark's Parish, the oldest of four children, and lived a relatively sheltered life; home, school and church played a major role in my upbringing. All that changed on Pearl Harbor Day as the young men in the area hastened to enlist in various branches of the armed forces.

My favorite date, Bob Tobin, joined the Army Air Corps and headed for California, delighted to have been selected into the cadets for pilot training. He wrote often, finally professing marriage as soon as he finished his training. Bob was commissioned a second lieutenant on December 5, 1943, and we were married on December 11 in our Parish Church. My life was never the same. I became a military dependent!

Our first assignment was in Del Rio, Texas, right on the Mexican border. We lived in a motel just outside the base. The men worked long hours, and the wives did volunteer work and socialized, getting to know each other. Six weeks later, we transferred to Shreveport, Louisiana, and more of the same. We were so young, and we knew our time together was short.

In April of 1944, I returned home as Bob and his company were on their way overseas, flying across the Atlantic in their own planes with their own crews—quite a thrill for a young man who had yet to drive a car! Bob spent six months in England and then went to France for the duration.

On Valentine's Day 1945, the casualties were heavy, and I was notified that Bob was missing in action; it was a very dark time in our lives. On Easter Sunday, I received the "good" news that he was a prisoner of war. He was liberated by the Americans and shipped to England for treatment. His left hand was burned, and he was very thin but recovered quickly and returned to Boston on the *Queen Elizabeth*, which had been converted to a troop carrier. Life resumed.

Our family time improved enormously. Assigned to Middletown, Pennsylvania, we made wonderful friends. Our children arrived periodically, healthy and beautiful, but after five years, Bob was at the top of the Overseas Assignment List. My personal choices were Paris and London, in that order, but the air force decided the Alaskan Air Command was a priority.

Alaska had not been made a state in 1951 and housing was tight, so the children and I returned home until quarters become available. My family moved over to make room for us, and again we waited. Eventually, I received the okay to make travel arrangements. I was issued a briefcase full of vouchers, orders, and suggestions, and proceeded to make plans. We were to fly to Seattle, Washington, commercially, proceed to McChord AFB (in the area), and then continue our flight by military transportation to Anchorage. This was before Jets. With four children and the oldest being eight, it was no time for a breakdown. We did it.

My mother's main concern was our traveling wardrobe, as it was extremely important to make a good impression in order to receive good service. I found a dark blue silk suit, a white French felt hat, and the requisite white kid gloves. The girls were to wear gingham dresses guaranteed not to wrinkle, hats and gloves, of course, and Mary Jane shoes. Martha, who was only fourteen months old, wore a hand-smocked Polly Flinders dress and high white shoes. Bobby was easy, shorts and a polo shirt from Bests. We were ready. And the press was there to see us off! We were on the front page of the *Herald*'s Sunday morning edition under the headline "Hub Family off to Alaska."

We left Logan Airport on a rainy afternoon, landed in Chicago for a two-hour layover, and then got back on the plane for the long trip to Seattle. We had great seats, no first-class section, but the front of the plane had seats that faced each other and were quite roomy. The children slept all night. Amazing!

Bob met us in Seattle, settled us into a military hotel and went off to check our reservations for the next day. Unfortunately, someone had sent me the wrong information; the dependents flight had departed that day; there was a six-day wait for the next one. Bob made a few phone calls and got assigned as a third pilot on a cargo flight leaving the next morning; we were part of the cargo.

We got up early, dressed in our traveling clothes, and I took the children to breakfast while Bob found a cab driver willing to take us the fifty miles to the MATS (Military Air Transport Service) terminal. Bob kissed us good-bye and disappeared into the cockpit of the largest plane I had ever seen. A young man arrived from the hanger, announced he was our escort, and proceeded to give me orders!

Military rules required that we be "suitably dressed" in jeans or pants, shirts, sweaters, or jackets, so I unpacked and found clothes that would pass muster. And so we boarded. We were the only passengers. There were no seats, just canvas benches along the sides of the plane, similar to the benches paratroopers sit on while waiting to jump. The flight was a "garbage run," carrying fresh fruits and vegetables to the commissaries in Anchorage and Fairbanks. It was jammed with crates, and we had to be weighed to make sure it wasn't overloaded. It was quite an eye-opener, but also the best flight we ever had.

Our escort played games with the older children, and passed out books, puzzles, and drawing supplies while the baby and I had a nap in the captain's cabin. I was quite ready to adopt this amazing young man when he served hot tomato soup and grilled cheese sandwiches for lunch, and placed bowls of Hershey bars within reach. The pilot descended a bit so we could view the Mendenhall Glacier. It was unbelievably beautiful.

We arrived in Anchorage and were met by friends who were loaning us their second car while we waited for ours to arrive on the ferry. Our *Beverly Hillbillies* image was reinforced when the car turned out to be a classic Model A Ford, a collector's item. Our friend Bob Hasek informed us the insurance premium for the car was higher than his family plan. My husband was in seventh heaven; the car ran like a charm, and we were very grateful. I never drove it!

Our quarters were fine: a duplex house, snug, warm, and quite comfortable. We adapted to the quirks of Alaskan life, the brightness of the summer nights and the darkness in the winter. We fished for salmon in a local stream, went rowing on Green Lake, ice-skated in the play area between the houses, and coasted wherever the snow fell. The children played the same games they would have played at home. I belonged to a bridge club, a book club, and the Chapel Guild. The Officer's Club had a wonderful orchestra that played each weekend, and Bob and I seldom missed a dance. The men worked twelve-hour shifts on the flight line, three days on and three days off, but on their off days, they flew to Tokyo, Seattle, or Great Falls, Montana, weather permitting. We were busy.

Alaska is beautiful, and a thirty-minute ride in any direction could leave you breathless. Anchorage was still quite rural in our time, 1951–52. Just two streets were paved, and the catalogue center for Sears was the highlight of the downtown center. Because we brought our clothes with us, there was little need to shop. That was a good thing, as the merchants added the cost of shipping to every purchase bought off base, and it could get pricey.

The climate was a surprise. The summers were beautiful; the only thing we missed was the beach. And indoor swimming pools were nonexistent at that time. The winters were cold but clear; I don't remember any blizzards, the snow fell at night. And we dressed properly: hats, gloves, and boots. The children thrived in that environment; they never had colds, earaches, or sore throats. In the time we were there, I never had to take any of them to the doctor or dentist. We were extremely fortunate. It was a great assignment. I expect that the darkness in the winter months could become quite depressing in the long run, but knowing we were there for only a short time put everything in perspective.

Our tour ended on October 1, 1952. Bob had requested the Air Force Academy in Colorado (we had all the clothes!), but the air force, in its infinite wisdom, decided we were better suited to the charm of Maxwell AFB in Montgomery, Alabama. And that's another story!

When I Was a Lutheran

Edith Bargar

My husband, Marshall, and I were married in 1944 during World War II. He was a soldier stationed in Augusta, Georgia. It was several months before I could join him. When he was allowed to live off-base weekends, he started looking for a place for me to live, because, at that time, wives and family were not allowed to live on the army base.

His main objective was to be sure that I would be safe and comfortable and, secondly, at a convenient distance and in a pleasant area. I don't recall whether he found a room for me with a great family by answering an ad or by ringing doorbells.

We were so fortunate to be welcomed so warmly by the Baker family, consisting of mom, dad, and two adorable young children. I confess that it has been so many years since I've thought of them that I can't remember their names.

Before I met them, my husband cautioned me about his apprehension as to acknowledging our religion to the Bakers. At his meeting with Mrs. Baker, she emphasized the fact that they were a religious, churchgoing family. Worried that there might be some prejudice against Jews, Marshall lied about our faith and said that we were Lutherans. Knowing that the Bakers were Baptist, and that it was unlikely that there was a place for Lutherans to worship nearby, he felt that his lie was justified.

The following weekend when Marshall joined me, he spotted my little white prayer book on the mantelpiece in our room and immediately knew that I had confessed our dishonesty. When I explained my reasons for doing so, he understood why I did so. After just a few days of living with this wonderful family, I was positive that my disclosure would not be a problem, and I was so right. They really didn't have to, but they reassured me that our fears were unwarranted.

I lived with them so happily for several months, and I will always remember their tolerance, having learned that their feelings were not unique.

Boston Baseball Memories

Paul Leonard

I grew up in a Jewish section of Dorchester. My earliest childhood friends were Harold Gelstein and Jordan Hirschfield. We were the same age, but they attended the William Bradford School while I walked a mile each way to St. Matthew's. I was the "shabbas goy" who helped turn the lights on at one of the many synagogues in the neighborhood. Other boys would join us every day to play some kind of ball. Our games were called box ball, squash, stickball, and "baseball against." You probably have a good idea on the first three, but baseball against was a little different. A rubber ball was thrown against a hard-surfaced front stairs. You aimed at the point of the stair, and hoped it would land safely on the street, or even better, across the street in a neighbor's yard.

Games were interrupted when either Harold or "Jordy" were called into their home to study Hebrew. Also, a temporary delay occurred when a stray ball needed to be delicately fished out of a sewer with a broken-down coat hanger. To this day, I would recognize the odor you experienced when you were face to face with a sewer cover. You could live with the smell as long as you retrieved the precious ball.

At about age ten, we moved on to play hardball at Franklin Field. The baseball of choice was called a nickel brick. The cover of the ball lasted about two innings. Then the designated taper of the ball would do his thing. We now have designated hitters, but back then we had designated tapers. The shape of the ball tended to become more oval over time. The life of a ball lasted virtually forever as long as you had Dad's tape. Our most memorable games were against the "Americans" from Winston Road. I was particularly envious of that team because they wore red, white, and blue jackets with a large "A" on their chest.

Like many Dorchester boys, one of my most exciting baseball memories was my initial sight of Fenway Park. My older brother, Larry, a member of the Civilian Conservation Corps (FDR's "New Deal"), took me. My heart was pounding as I walked up Brookline Avenue and spotted the huge netting over the left field wall. It was a thrill entering the ballpark to see the lush green grass and what is now called the Green Monster. At that time, the wall was dotted with ads like Schenley Whiskey, Gemblades, and Lifebuoy Soap. Ted Williams, "The Splendid Splinter" was to arrive the next year in 1939. In 1938, the Sox had names like Doerr, Taber, Foxx, and Grove. Their player-manager was Joe Cronin.

In 1946, I skipped school at English High to see a World Series game between the Sox and the St. Louis Cardinals. The Sox were led by the likes of Pesky, DiMaggio, and, of course, Ted Williams. The Cardinals featured future Hall of Famer Stan Musial. I bought a ticket the day of the game. I still have the stub; the price was $1.25. The Cardinals won in seven games on Enos Slaughter's eighth inning "mad dash" from first base that gave them a 4–3 lead. In 1949, while playing for the St. Matthew's CYO team, I was fortunate to play two games at Fenway. Two Milton residents were on that team. Their names are Eddie Miller and Bob Macomber. The best player on the team was probably Vin Milano. One of his drives just missed going over the Monster. He has a cousin with the same name currently living at Fuller Village.

In 1960, I saw one of the most memorable home runs at that "lyric little bandbox of a ballpark," Fenway Park. It was a dark, dreary day almost fifty years ago when Ted Williams, in the last at bat of his storied career, hit a home run off of Jack Fisher of the Orioles. As John Updike reported, I was privileged to be among the few "hub fans to bid the kid adieu." A close friend, Bernie Curley (another great ballplayer, by the way) and I validate our presence at the game along with the other 9,500 faithful fans who saw Ted in his last at bat.

On a steamy Friday night in 1967, along with two of my children, I witnessed a tragedy as Boston's own Tony Conigliaro got beaned by Jack Hamilton of the Angels. Tony was carried off on a stretcher. He came back in 1969 but was never the same. Unfortunately, he died a young man.

Lastly, a few months ago I was at Fenway to see my grandson, John Leonard of Boston College, pitch for the prestigious Cape Cod League All Stars. It was great to see him in a Red Sox uniform under the lights. It may have been a Yarmouth-Dennis Red Sox uniform, but it was close enough! Unfortunately, rain shortened the game and John was prevented from pitching off the Fenway mound. Hopefully, he'll get a chance in the future.

My poor vision now precludes me from attending Red Sox games at Fenway. However, I can still watch games with my nose on the TV screen while rooting for my beloved Red Sox. Nothing can erase my vivid memories of growing up playing ball in Dorchester and my happy trips to Fenway Park. In addition, I have many other memories of Dorchester and Boston, but that will have to be another story for another day.

Shiny, Red Patent

Nancy Kearns

Shiny red patent-leather shoes, a flowered china teacup and saucer, and gently worn crystal rosary beads. At Nonie Sullivan's Funeral Mass, these items were reverently brought to the altar by her grandchildren. Each of the ten spoke of Nana, bringing smiles and happy tears to those in the hushed congregation.

Nora Rita O'Sullivan was born in a small village in County Kerry Ireland. She was my amazing mother who married my wonderful Dad, Peter Sullivan, from the fishing village of Bantry, County Cork. They raised four robust, happy children in a "two-decker" in Dorchester in St. Brendan's Parish. She always had a twinkle in her eye and would often advise, "Keep the good side out."

Nonie loved to dance, especially to lively Irish music. This is why we chose the shiny red pair of shoes as one representation. She would often wear them on Sunday nights as she met her dear friends at the Irish Social Club in West Roxbury. In her twenties, as a sometimes-homesick colleen, she and her friends would meet the lads and dance the night away at Hibernian Hall on Dudley Street in Roxbury. The music, dance, and friendship were reminiscent of their innocent gatherings in the pubs back home. Later in life, Nonie would beckon to one of her children, and we'd dance a spirited polka around the kitchen floor.

The kettle was always on the stove, simmering away, ready to make a cup of tea often served with her homemade Irish bread; certainly not just for St. Patrick's Day! Every visitor was greeted with warm hospitality, morning, noon, or night. Many were the times I watched Nonie mix the ingredients in her large, yellow ceramic bowl. Her Irish bread had no written recipe. Instead it was just a fistful of flour and a pinch of soda, baked in a round cast-iron pan. As she took it from the oven, she'd breathe a sigh of relief and say, "Thank God it came out alright!"

Nonie's faith in God was always present and very powerful. Daily Mass, kneeling in the kitchen to pray the rosary with Cardinal Cushing's radio broadcast, and attending novenas were a part of Nonie and Pete's comfortable routine. It was a part of their children's lives, seldom to be questioned. My brother, Rev. John Sullivan is a LaSalette priest. Nonie was very proud of all of her children. But we used to chuckle at the speed with which the phrase "my son the priest" was interjected into conversations with everyone she met! Come to think of it, I do the same and all my friends know of "my brother the priest."

Love of music and dance, laughter, generosity, hospitality, and an ever-present faith providing strength and hope through life's inevitable trials are all integral parts of Nonie's legacy. I am blessed to have inherited many of these amazing gifts, and I hope I have passed them on to my children.

As I conclude my musing, I pose a question to the readers of this book of fascinating memoirs. What might be the ingredients of your legacy? Are they subtle or obvious? Do your children and grandchildren see you as you see yourself? Perhaps one day, you'll have the opportunity to ask them how you'll be remembered, and it may be the beginning of a wonderful conversation.

Ireland Comes to America

Francis P. McDermott

The saga of the McDermott family began in 1847, when my great-granduncle Timothy McDermott came to the United States from County Roscommon, Ireland, and settled in Milton. I am a fourth-generation Miltonian. Timothy had seven children; the firstborn was my grand- uncle. Timothy was chief of the Milton Police Department (1934–1936). He retired after forty-six years of service. His brother Frank was a Milton patrolman for thirty-three years.

Frank had a son named Thomas Joseph, who is my father. Unfortunately, Thomas developed a kidney disease and died at the early age of thirty-six, leaving a widow and three children: me, age seven, my sister, Betty, age three, and my brother, John, age two. My father had a good job as a cable splicer with the telephone company, but as luck would have it, he died just before social security became available. As a result, my mother had to seek employment and did so by getting her old job back with the telephone company. However, she was forced to work split shifts, a burden on a woman with three children under seven.

My mother, who came from Carbonear, Newfoundland, was an extremely intelligent woman. If she had had an education, she would have become a great financier. It was amazing what she could do with a dollar.

My early years were spent at the Milton town field on Brook Road, where I spent time with other boys whose families did not have summer places. Perhaps because of the boredom, I became interested in the game of checkers and became the checkers champ. I would feel I had died and gone to heaven when my grandmother invited me for a week at Rocky Nook in Kingston.

After Tucker school and Milton Junior High, I attended Boston College High School. This led me to a freshman year at

Boston College. After one year, I had enough of school, so I joined the navy.

After boot camp, I volunteered for the submarine service as I heard you got an 80 percent bonus for being in the submarines. When they found out I couldn't tie a knot, they directed me to Control Operators School in Jacksonville, Florida. I guess they figured I had enough intelligence to tell a plane to land and take off, so they made me a control tower operator.

They didn't tell me about the stress associated with the job, so much stress that you had twenty-four hours off for every four that you worked. It was a hell of a job for a kid seventeen years old. For example, it was a bit earth-shaking when an aircraft carrier sent all its planes to Quonset Point, Rhode Island, where I was stationed. The first you would hear would be the leader of the group with the call sign "Wife Beater Number One" request landing instructions for a flock of sixty planes, and then they would all land three abreast rather than one by one. We prayed no one would blow a tire.

Of course, nothing could match a plane asking permission to land when the ceiling was about four hundred feet and the radar was not working properly because of thunder and lightning, and the pilot says he's running out of fuel. The 50 percent bonus (called flight skins) for being in the Navy Air Corps didn't seem to be enough for the tension of the job. I survived and was discharged in 1948 as an air controlman 3rd class. I reentered Boston College and graduated in 1952. I am one of a number of past presidents of that class.

In 1949, you had to be twenty-one years old to vote or get elected to political office. I had just turned twenty-one in 1949 and ran for office as a town meeting member and was lucky to get elected. I forget now, but there may have been ten people running for ten slots. If there were eleven running, I might have lost. In any event, I think I was the youngest to be elected at the age of twenty-one.

During the summers, I worked as a landscaper in Harwichport on Cape Cod. I was given the name "Pine Needles" because I would go into the public woods and rake up a truck load of pine needles, rent a truck and driver, and sell the needles to people who had pine trees but no needles on their lawn. It was a profitable business, but I was a young, virile youth, and I began to date the waitresses at the New York

Restaurant and the Melrose Inn in Harwichport; as luck would have it, they went home with all their earnings, and I went home broke. Thank God for Public Law 346 where the federal government gave $75.00 per month to college students who had served in the military.

At Boston College, I majored in finance and hoped to become a stock analyst. But in 1952, there was a recession, and I was lucky to get a job as a claims adjuster. It was there that a fellow claims adjuster introduced me to Dorothy Davock, a girl too beautiful for the likes of me, but who, after a rather intense courtship, agreed to marry me. She was and is a great wife, mother, and companion and was a real asset to me as I strove to make my mark in life. While our six children were in their teens, I bought a twenty-six-foot Lyman and named it the *Dorothy J.* It was a great source of joy as we traveled the waters around Boston and Cape Cod.

Trials & Tribulations of a Court in Transition

Eugene G. Panarese

On December 8, 1988, Gov. Michael Dukakis appointed me presiding justice of the Chelsea District with jurisdiction covering Chelsea and Revere. The court was housed in a one-hundred-year-old building with the police station at ground level, a courtroom on the first and second floors, and a prisoners' lock-up in the basement. Conditions on all levels were deplorable: private files in the hallway exposed to public viewing, a stairway to the second floor so narrow that in the event of fire, the ensuing tragedy would mimic that of the infamous Coconut Grove disaster of the 1940s, insufferable summer heat without air conditioning and, most grievously, a prisoners' lock-up with cells encased in sheets of half inch thick plastic. I ordered holes to be drilled into the plastic allowing at least some circulation of air.

In 1992, I successfully petitioned the city building inspector to condemn the obsolete structure, and I simultaneously obtained an order by our supreme judicial court to "cease operation forthwith." The court was temporarily relocated to one in East Cambridge. Remarkably, over one weekend, the entire court operation was seamlessly transitioned!

With the advent of jury trials in the district courts, cases from Brighton, East Boston, and Charlestown came under our jurisdiction. The increased workload was not balanced with additional personnel to handle the logistical, financial, and personal hardships imposed upon litigants, witnesses, and others with matters before the court.

In March of 2000, the court returned to a newly constructed state-of-the-art courthouse in Chelsea. The temporary Cambridge displacement had lasted eight years! Regrettably, on August 21, 1998 (my seventieth birthday), mandatory retirement deprived me of the fulfillment of my dream to sit in the new courthouse.

Too old! Too soon! But what a glorious ride!

Candled Eggs and Herring

Saul Buchbinder

My family lived in East Boston in the late 1930s where my father owned a neighborhood produce store. To buy his produce, he needed to go to the market district in Boston, and so he would get up at 4:00 AM. to get the early street Massachusetts Transit Authority (MTA) into town. It became my responsibility, at 5:00 AM, to take our horse and wagon and go by ferry to meet him. There was no Sumner Tunnel at that time.

I would get the horse from the stable located a mile from our house and then follow an unchanging routine: I walked the horse to the water tub so that he could take a drink, after which I put the harness on him and attached him to the wagon. We then went to meet the ferry that would take us over to Boston. When we arrived in Boston (State Street) I would drop the bit from his mouth and put the feed bucket strap over his head so that he could have his breakfast. In the winter, my father prepared a loaf of bread for the horse that was soaked in home-made wine and this warmed him up for our morning trip. I secured his blanket before we started out of the barn. I brought him to the market district where my father always picked him up with the fruit and vegetables that he had already purchased for the store.

After leaving the horse and wagon for my father, I took the MTA back home, had breakfast, and went off to school. On one occasion when my father got to the horse, he had no blanket over him, so my father took off his own warm jacket and put it over the horse's back. My father always took care of his animals first, and he thought I had forgotten to put the blanket over the horse.

The next day, a citation came from the court with a date for my father to come to court to explain why the horse had nothing over him on such a cold morning. It was considered animal cruelty. We went to court with two sales slips proving that he had indeed purchased horse blankets, and the one over the horse had obviously been stolen that morning. My father preferred to be cold himself rather than have the animal suffer. The judge smiled, thanked my father, and dismissed the case!

We sold fruit and vegetables and other staples that did not require refrigeration; the store had no refrigeration. We did carry eggs, however, which made it convenient for the neighbors. But eggs, without being refrigerated, could and did go bad. I was fascinated by my father's ingenuity, as out of necessity, he found a way to differentiate the good eggs from those he would not be able to sell.

I watched as he developed his own system of "candling." The process included a board on which he mounted a candle. He would then cut a hole in the bottom of an empty coffee can to fit an egg. At that point he lit a candle and then placed the coffee can over the candle. Then he would place the egg over the hole. If the egg had a dark shadow, it was discarded. It was a creative method of checking inventory.

I remember the large barrel at the front of the store from which he would sell schmaltz herring every Saturday. He had a great many customers who came in weekly for this "delicacy." I would watch him roll up the sleeves of his shirt, put his arm into the barrel, swirl his arm round and round, and finally bring up a herring. The customer would examine the fish and, if it was satisfactory, the sale was made. If it was not satisfactory, my father would drop the herring back into the barrel and bring up another fish until the customer was satisfied.

One late Saturday evening as we were ready to leave the store and go home, a woman came running in for her schmaltz herring. I knew there was only one fish left and we were going to wrap it up ourselves to have for Sunday morning breakfast with candled eggs. But my father, the entrepreneur, preferred to make a sale. He performed as always, hand in the barrel, going round and round and finally coming up with the herring. But the customer did not like that particular herring, and so my father repeated his performance. He came up with the same herring and the customer said, "No." Once again he dropped the herring into the barrel, swished it around, and came up with the very same herring. The customer said, "Okay, that looks good. I'll take it!"

(Top L to R) Jerry Joyce, Myrtle Flight
Betsy and Saul Buchbinder
(Seated) Jan Tobin, Agnes Walker
Josephine Accattatis

Remembering the Depression Era

Betsy Buchbinder

I do not remember feeling poor, nor do I remember feeling unhappy as a child during that period of time history now depicts as "The Depression Era."

But I do remember vividly that my father was unemployed then and that my grandmother and aunt came to live with us in our small apartment. It was of financial necessity that our family structure changed, but, for me as an only child, it seemed wonderful having relatives living with us. We became four adults and one child living in a two-bedroom flat. It was many years later that I realized what intense pressures my family had to contend with that forced such a choice.

As a youngster in those Depression Era days, I knew nothing about the worldwide implications of the time, of the widespread poverty and unemployment, nor could I understand the cataclysmic financial pressures on families like my own. But, many years later in retrospect, it became clear as I realized the full impact those years had on all our lives.

I remember that on our street were many families with children of all ages who played together, walked to school together, and shared clothing—more specifically shoes as we grew out of a particular size. One of the houses at the top of the street had a wraparound porch, and it served as the place where still-wearable shoes were dropped off for other families to pick from as needed. As I grew, my mother simply replaced my shoes with a "new" pair from the "Shoe Box" up the street. Many of the mothers had sewing machines, and so other types of clothing were made and altered as needed. But shoes had to be exchanged! A sad consequence took place many years later when I had to have a small toe amputated, a toe that had been squeezed tightly for so many years into too-small shoes.

I remember that at 10:30 every winter evening my mother woke me, handed me a warm sweater, and we went down together to the basement where we were joined by our neighbors. A single lightbulb hung from the ceiling while we stoked the furnaces, and everyone put back into their furnace the bigger hunks of red-hot coal that had fallen out so that not a single coal that was still worth using again was ever wasted. It was a winter ritual that I actually thought was fun, being up at night with my friends in the building, feeling useful.

My family was among those whose lives were impacted by circumstances well beyond their control. But, as I remember some of the deprivations, I realize that overcoming difficulties can often serve to be a source of strength. I now buy shoes when I choose to, and I make certain they fit properly! I raise and lower the heat by a thermostat. My family and I survived intact, possibly even stronger for the challenges. So I can revisit those memories with appreciation for what is now!

Home Is Where the Heart Is—Army Style

Catherine Gilligan

I grew up in the small town of Clinton, Massachusetts, in the western part of the state. I lived there during the Depression of 1929 and the hurricane of 1938, after which I went to nursing school in February 1939. The United States was getting involved in World War II.

Graduating after three years of twelve-hour duty (the norm in those days), two classmates and I headed to the big city of Boston. We were going to Boston Lying-in Hospital for a six-month course in obstetrics to further our education in that field.

Because of the war and a shortage of nurses, we were asked to join the nursing staff for a few months and live in the nurses' quarters. At twenty-one years of age, it sounded inviting, especially because we'd be living next door to the Harvard medical students' dormitory.

After six months, two of us left, intending to enlist in the army or navy. But as soon as I arrived home, another classmate called to say she was going to Fort Devens in Ayer. Lovell General Hospital was the army hospital on the base, and I decided to accompany her.

We were required to take a civil service exam and a physical, in addition to having our references checked and our fingerprints taken. We were interviewed by the chief nurse, an army major, and were hired that day. We were ordered to report for duty the following Monday.

Upon arriving for our first day of duty, we were shown our assigned wards, empty at the time except for beds and tables. We were told to take charge of a "ward boy" (in my case, a private by the name of Sam), a cadet nurse, two aides, and a secretary. The nurse, aides, and secretary were civil service employees.

For those unfamiliar with barracks, which these wards were, let me explain. The entrance to the hospital was in the center of this long, one-story building that spread out on each side. As I recall, it was constructed by army engineers. From the center, each side had a long corridor, and the barracks or wards each ran from this corridor. I've forgotten how many there were. Each barrack was a separate ward. Some of these were for X-ray equipment, records, therapy, and PX, as well as for patients. There was a mess hall for serving meals to civil service employees and army personnel.

Our ward (after you entered from the corridor) had four private rooms, the doctor's office, the nurse's office, an examining room, a treatment room with medicine cabinets, a laundry room, and a locker room for patients' belongings and clothes. Only the ward boy and nurse had keys to the lockers. This was army regulation; I was in the army now! Then you stepped into the large ward holding forty beds, twenty on each side of the room. There was a large porch at the back end with a large double door in the back, through which the patients would be admitted. There was another side porch equipped with a ping-pong table, card tables, a radio, some games like checkers and chess. There was no TV or electronic games in those days.

Beds were made and everything was scrubbed and cleaned to pass an army-style white-glove inspection. Ward 41 was open for business. What a day that was! We got ready to receive the ambulances and buses that would deliver our patients who had been en route from a hospital in England. It was a very exciting day—one that I've never forgotten—definitely not the usual hospital routine.

The patients came in from the back porch; some were ambulatory, some on crutches, some on stretchers with partially healed wounds, two with shell shock, a few with tuberculosis, some with foot disorders from wearing wet boots too long, and, surprisingly, two Italian prisoners of war who were placed in private rooms.

Seeing these soldiers in this condition was very sad, but, at the same time, the atmosphere was exhilarating. The soldiers were very excited to be back in the United States and one step closer to home. They had many questions, especially anticipating family visits after they were admitted, so the location of the telephones was first on their list. There were no cell phones in those days, but for patients' and employees' convenience, a barracks near the PX was fitted with many open booths and stools managed by AT&T employees.

The soldiers wanted to know where the PX was, when the doctor would see them, whether they could expect a weekend pass in the near future, how visitors could reach them, and where they could get something to eat. Every soldier was happy but also very concerned and serious about his own welfare and future.

They were all from different units, mostly infantry and from upstate New York, Connecticut, Rhode Island, Massachusetts, New Hampshire, and Maine. A few knew one another. Eventually, they all found a pal who was compatible, whether it was because they liked to play cards, enjoyed music, or came from the same state or town; that's what their life had been for the last few years—making new friends. Everyone had settled down by the time I left at 5:00 P.M. when the night nurse came on duty.

I had a couple of extremely busy days and weeks getting into a normal nursing routine, which began with teams of doctors making rounds as each patient was evaluated. Referrals were made to dentists, surgeons, psychiatrists, and therapists. Patients had to be sent to different services and records and charts kept up to date. Patients were also being discharged or were given weekend passes during treatment. Some were being sent back to active duty; that was not the favorite solution.

It was an experience I've never forgotten. I enjoyed being part of the happier side of the war: the coming-home side. I was on duty there when my future husband came home uninjured. We met by appointment in the PX, and I brought him home to announce to my parents that we were getting married in ten days. That was in 1945. The rest I'll save for my book.

That Fateful Day

John J. "Jack" McCarthy

I was not yet a member of the LST 912 crew when she was hit by a Japanese Kamikaze plane. On January 8, 1945, I was in the wheelhouse of the LST 910, which was in line formation behind the LST 912. As a quartermaster, my general quarters (G.Q.) station was in the wheelhouse. This gave me a clear view of what was happening. We were being attacked by so many Japanese planes on that day and the next three days that they seemed to be coming from all directions. In that four-day period, we were called to G.Q. thirty-six times.

On the morning of January 8, 1945, a Japanese dive bomber came from our port side; it may have been hit, as it looked like it was trailing smoke. It slammed into the stern gun tub of the LST 912, causing four crewmembers to die and eight to be wounded. A fire ensued but was put out by the damage control team before any ammunition exploded. The LST 910 was astern in line, with one other LST in-between.

Loyola Vuolo, the wife of my shipmate Pat Vuolo, condensed the Log Book of the LST 910. She was kind enough to copy her notes and send them to me in January 2005. Here are the excerpts from the pages of her notes of that event. As with all of the ship's logs, they are very sterile. They do not go into detail as to what was happening around us, which other ships were with us, and their type. Nor do they go into the reaction of the crew and what affect it had on them.

"5 January 1945: assumed position 1-4 in convoy. Started fog machine. Commencing at dusk on 5 January 1945 air alerts were frequent. The use of artificial fog was frequently directed by the OTC.

7 January 1945: Air Raid, Night fighting. Japanese Destroyer sunk.

8 January 1945: 0247 sounded G.Q. 0320 started fog machine. 0530 Convoy attacked from all angles by enemy planes. Open fired with gun 40-6 on plane overhead. Passing from port to starboard very low. LST 912 hit on stern by enemy suicide dive-bomber coming in from 1510 degrees (t). LST 912 set afire. LST9I0 passed burning wreckage of dive-bomber abeam to port, distance 50 yards. Changed convoy speed to 9.5 knots. 0758 fired at enemy plane passing across our bow from port to starboard after same plane dropped a small bomb off our port bow a distance of 200 yards. Jap plane dove into APA 35 USS Callaway *in column one of transport formation. APA 35 set afire. LST 910 changed course. Secured from G.Q. 0900.*

NOTE: From Action Report #108682—On January 8,1945 Task Group 78.5 was under intermittent attack from 0247 to 0912. At 0545 January 8, 1945 LST 912, two ships ahead of this vessel in column, was struck by a suicide Japanese plane. At 0758 January 8,1945 opened fire on a Japanese Zero who dropped a small bomb about 100 yards off our port bow then crossed over the ship. No hits observed. About 0800 8 January 1945 suicide plane dove into USS Callaway. During this period a CVE in rear of formation was bombed.

Half-mast colors; stood by for burial at sea. Funeral services held on APA 35 seven men; LST 912 four men.

9 January 1945: Ship 4th in 2nd column, astern LST 777. Anchored in Lingayen Gulf. Crew to G.Q. twice. Opened fire on one Jap Betty passing overhead from port bow to the starboard quarter. NOTE From Action Report #108682 - Anchored in outer LST area, Lingayen Gulf at 0800 on 9 January 1945 to await call into Blue Beach One. Our 21st beaching. Air alerts continued. 1858 opened fire on Japanese Betty passing overhead from port to starboard. No hits observed as plane was high."

Wine Making Home-Style

Josephine Accattatis

In the early 1900s, many of the Italian families who had emigrated to the United States would make their own wine. It was an interesting process, and it yielded wonderful wine.

My husband, Frank, who had come to the United States in 1947 from the city of Rome, had never had the experience of participating in this home wine making process in Italy, but he was initiated into this process with my family. Frank was excited by the prospect of making wine at home, and my father thought we would have fun as well as wine with this experience Frank was about to have with us.

As we waited for the delivery truck with the cases of red and white grapes to arrive at our house, my dad looked at me and gave a big wink. I knew we would indeed have fun and wine! After the cases of grapes arrived, my dad started to explain what each of us were to do, what jobs we were assigned to in the wine making process. I didn't know what to expect.

My father explained that, at first, the grapes were to be put into a crusher that resembled a large meat grinder set on top of a barrel. After several days of fermentation, the wine is then put into another barrel, and the grapes are transferred to the wine press. It was fun so see what looked like grape juice pouring out of the wine press.

Now it became Frank's role to clean out the crushed grapes from the barrel and transfer them to the press. While doing this particular job, Frank's head was pretty much immersed in the barrel. While he was bent over the barrel with his head inside, he continued to breathe and, of course, breathed in the fumes—the wine.

It is not hard to imagine what happened to Frank; he became tipsy. There was no more home wine making for him ever again!

A Navy Pilot's World War II Experience

Alfred J. Hall

In 1939, I lived in Tuckahoe, New York, and was a student at Eastchester High School. In my junior year, I signed up for the naval reserve because I wanted to play basketball. We traveled around the country trying to get people to enlist in the navy. After graduation in June of 1941, I received a terrible notice: "Please report for duty." At first I was an aviation mechanic, and then they asked for volunteers to work in the control tower. In a short period of time, I became qualified to direct all air traffic for the FAA and anyone else. I had just turned nineteen, and my commander encouraged me to go to flight school.

I then started a long series of training classes from Chapel Hill, North Carolina, to Lake Michigan, San Diego, California, Oregon, and the desert (El Centro) for night flying. I was assigned to the *Bismarck Sea*, an aircraft carrier built by Kaiser. It was four hundred feet long: two hundred feet for landing and two hundred feet to take off. It was forty-eight feet wide and the flight deck was forty-seven feet above the water. We headed for Pearl Harbor after getting acquainted with the ship. After we got to Pearl Harbor, we were informed we were going to Alaska—to run the Japanese out of Alaska. We celebrated Christmas on some island. There was always a discussion of how many islands we had to take: Saipan, Guam, Guadalcanal, the Philippines, and Iwo Jima were named the most often. Eventually, we arrived in Iwo Jima.

On the twenty-first of February, 1945, I was aboard the USS *Bismarck Sea* CVE 95 in fighter squadron VC86. We were operating fifty to seventy miles off the coast of Iwo Jima, providing close air support for the marines who had landed on the nineteenth of February. Jack Wouters and I were on a late afternoon routine flight to scan the returning American task force aircraft. We had to be sure no Japanese airplanes were trailing our return flights. At about 6:30 PM, we landed aboard the *Bismarck Sea*, unaware we were the last two fighter pilots who would ever do so.

Minutes after we entered the ready room, the ship was struck on the aft starboard side by a kamikaze. I went to the flight deck, assuming Jack was following me. As it turned out, I wasn't to see him until four hours later. I tried to assist two seamen with a heavy fire hose to put out the fire, but there was no water pressure. Again we were hit by a second kamikaze in the aft elevator. Within minutes, the announcement came to abandon ship.

Fortunately, I had never had time to take off my life jacket. I went forward on the flight deck, climbed into the cockpit of a plane and pulled the one-man life raft from the parachute. Continuing forward, I lowered myself to the forecastle where there was a large group discussing who would go first. I volunteered and went to the starboard side where I could see "monkey lines." As I was going hand over hand down a line, I heard my name called from the forecastle; it was A. J. Jones. I climbed back on the ship, and we checked each other's life jackets, making sure they were properly harnessed. I started down the line first, with the one-man raft tucked under one arm. A. J. followed, but I never saw him again once we hit the water. I fully intended to swim nine thousand miles to San Francisco.

I swam several yards from the ship, inflated my life raft, and attached its safety line to my belt. Since the wind was blowing upwards of twenty knots and the waves were ten to fifteen feet high, the raft floated away from me. People grabbed for the raft and tried to board it. I pulled myself toward the raft, made the one person in the raft get out, and told everyone to form two circles, the inner one to hold on to the raft and the outer one to hold on to the shoulders of those holding on to the raft. I counted eleven men, none of whom I recognized at first. I was the twelfth but was not holding on to the raft.

We moved away from the ship and tried to turn our backs into the waves and drift. I then identified one person whom we helped on the raft, the ship's chaplain, Lieutenant Shannon, who was severely wounded. We floated for about three hours. Periodically on top of a wave, I would hold a flashlight I had taken from one of the seamen on the raft and hold it about my head. Finally, we heard a voice on a ship's bullhorn say, "We see you. We will pick you up shortly." We continued to float downwind close to the bow of this destroyer, the U.S.S. *Edmonds*. Lines were thrown to us, and I was able to grab one and pull us alongside the starboard side. There was a cargo net hanging down, and sailors from the destroyer were helping our men climb aboard.

Since I had both lines (ship and raft) and the ship was tolling heavily, I was being forced under water, partially under the ship and then jerked out of the water as the ship rolled again. This occurred three or four times, and I was exhausted. I saw the raft was empty, and on the next upward swing I unhooked the raft and grabbed the cargo net. Several people reached down and hoisted me up. Once on deck, I was told to find dry clothes from a donated pile, get below, and find a bunk to sleep in. I entered a stateroom with four bunks, one of which was empty. Lo and behold, sound asleep in one lower bunk was Jack Wouters!

The next afternoon, after a burial at sea of our fallen comrades, Lieutenant Shannon included, we were transferred to an Attack Transport (APA) just off the beach at Iwo Jima. We thankfully watched the American flag being raised by the marines on Mt. Suribachi. A total of five hundred sailors were lost, including five aviators. All the survivors left Iwo Jima the following day on a transport to Saipan. There we met other survivors from the *Bismarck*. By many means—ships or planes—we were transported to Hawaii. There we were medically examined, given uniforms (some fit!), and money. I finally was able to call my parents who knew about the sinking but had been assured that all the next of kin had been notified.

After a long trip on a damaged transport, we arrived in San Diego and flew home on Easter Sunday. I enjoyed thirty days survivors' leave before I reported to Jackson-ville Naval Air Station for duty. The Pacific War ended in August, and D. J. and I were married in October. For the next twenty years, I was a naval aviator career officer. We still have reunions with many of the men. Some time ago each of us contributed a story of our recollections to a booklet entitled *Yearbook of Survivors*. What you read above was my most vivid recollection.

Our Family Follows the Fleet

Dorothy J. "DJ" Hall

Growing up in Scarsdale, New York, was a happy experience. I had many friends my age in the neighbor-hood. After college, things changed drastically. In 1945, I married my high school beau, Al Hall. He was a navy pilot who had flown off carriers in the South Pacific in World War II. He had then accepted a permanent navy commission.

As a background to my unique experience, I have to explain that in those days all carrier pilots had to spend six months at sea every few years. Al had previously deployed in 1953 to the Mediterranean, and I had followed the ship, leaving my sainted mother in care of our two daughters, then ages five and two. A month later, I called mother from Cannes, France, and stated that I had fifty dollars left and would like to go to Barcelona. She replied, "Come home immediately." So I did. I'll never know how she managed, and I'll always be grateful.

Now it is 1959, and Al is scheduled for another Mediterranean cruise. Again I called mother to ask if she would take the girls once more. Debby is now eleven and Katy eight. After a long pause I heard "Why don't I go with you, and we'll take the girls?" I agreed and away we went, landing in Genoa, Italy, after a week on the USS *Independence*.

On board ship, I had fortuitously met Ann Hessel, the wife of the captain of Al's ship, the USS *Roosevelt*. She was also traveling to join her husband. This was a made-in-heaven coincidence because, from then on, Captain Hessel sent his gig (personal motorboat) into shore every time we wanted to go aboard the ship for dinner. This was almost every time the ship was in port. The girls had not acquired international taste buds but loved the milk and mashed potatoes on the ship, and the movie of their choice afterward. Poor Al rarely ate ashore. He always said he was the only commanding officer in the navy who had a mother-in-law and two children following him from port to port!

Our first misadventure after reaching Genoa was picking up the Volkswagen Al had bought in advance. Debby, who had become my valued helper, had to draw a picture of a luggage rack Al had paid for. It was not installed, but it became installed. We were now traveling, Debby reading maps, me driving, Mother and Katy in the backseat surrounded by many bottles of water that mother insisted on buying.

Pisa was our first stop. Mother and I sat on a bench while the girls climbed the leaning tower. At the top, Debby instructed Katy to duck under the bell so that she could take a picture. Picture taken, Katy stood up and cracked her head open on the bell. Blood cascaded everywhere. A wonderful young Italian man carried her down, saying something like, "Opital." We followed him running to a hospital about four blocks away. Her head was shaved and stitched. I offered money for repairs to our bloodstained savior, but he refused. That night we saw Al for the first time in four months. "What happened to her?" was our greeting. Eventually, she healed and we continued on with more exciting adventures.

The *Roosevelt* had a cocktail party in Cannes, serving only nonalcoholic punch for many French and Italian dignitaries. Since Ann Hessel was crippled from childhood polio and was unable to stand in a receiving line, Captain Hessel asked me to be a surrogate hostess. I vividly remember meeting the young Aga Khan from Harvard.

To shorten this narrative, I'll just say I drove five thousand miles, mostly in Italy and France. Al took leave, and we went to Paris and parts of Switzerland. All of the languages were problems. My high school French and college Spanish were insufficient. Mother created more confusion by trying to talk and order meals. She would act out sentences as though playing charades. I remember her flying around a drugstore in Paris and pinching herself. A bored salesgirl said in English, "Do you want mosquito repellent?" Meals, except aboard the ship, were always a gamble. We never had overnight accommodations in advance because the ship's schedule kept being revised. We stayed mostly in modest pensiones (to overstate them) not four-star hotels. The bath was always down the hall.

Mother and Katy were saturated after six weeks and flew home. Debby and I stayed another six weeks and tackled Germany. We saw the *Passion Play* in Oberammergau. Sitting on a hard wooden bench for two long days was crippling. I understand the play has been shortened and the benches cushioned since then. We saw Ludwig's castles, etc. I had to drive at least eighty miles an hour on the autobahn. I never did have what every guard at every border asked for a "carte verde." However, I looked hopeless, shed a tear or two, and they let us pass.

On reaching home in Jacksonville in September, and after buying school uniforms, Al was transferred to Rhode Island. So it goes!

(L to R) Herbert Colcord, Al and DJ Hall and Henry Hanley

China—Twenty Years Outside Looking In

Anne N. Gebhardt

When China opened its borders to foreigners in the 1970s, it was soon woefully obvious they were far behind in most areas, from simple management to high technologies and health care. Their relationship with the Russians had not provided them the ability to keep abreast of their Western counterparts. The "barefoot doctors" of the Cultural Revolution were selected without regard to knowledge and were put in charge of the health needs of an area without any training, while the trained and skilled medical and surgical members, along with other highly educated professionals, were sent to the countryside to help the farmers.

Eventually, delegations were sent to the United States and other countries for observation and education. Surgeons, especially, soon realized that learning new procedures was challenging, but to put them into practice was difficult. There was no qualified nursing care available. There had been no teaching for thirty years, and the educated nurses were beyond retirement age. Most nurses now were high school graduates without any special health care training.

The Chinese wrote to the Peter Bent Brigham Hospital requesting an educational observation period for a Chinese nurse. The decision rested with the assistant director for staff education—as she would be planning the program—and me, the assistant director for clinical services, where the candidate would have most of her experience. We both were excited about such a program. My only request was that the candidate have a reasonable knowledge and use of the English language. We also offered to take care of living accommodations. At that time, the Chinese had not selected a candidate, but said they would keep us informed.

In 1980, the assistant director for staff education (Susan) and I were scheduled to go to Tokyo for an international conference. When the Chinese heard that, they invited us to China to have a dialogue with nurses in Beijing and Nanjing. Of course, we accepted. This would be the first official exchange with Western nurses! Even though we were officially invited, we had to enter China with a tour group; the Chinese were not yet ready to handle independent travelers. We had one other person with us, Kathryn, a research associate, who elected to participate in the program. While we were in Tokyo, the Chinese sent a delegation from Beijing to meet with us and assure us that we would be well cared for when in China.

After orientation in Hong Kong, we set off, entering China at Shenzhen. At customs, everything was inspected. I happened to be carrying textbooks, gifts for the two nursing departments. The inspector went through the books carefully. Although he could not read English, he found that some of the illustrations would not pass censorship and was not going to let me pass. He had three alternatives: ban me and the books, tear out the offending pages, or confiscate the books. Finally his superior allowed me to enter with the educational textbooks intact.

We traveled by hydrofoil up the Pearl River to Canton on our way to Shanghai. The decks, fore and aft, were lined with chairs. We were told to sit and not move, and no pictures! Soldiers, with guns aimed, guarded both decks.

Eventually, our tour group arrived in Shanghai where we were scheduled to stay several days. Here we would try to leave the tour and travel to Nanjing, a five-hour train ride. Since Nanjing was a different province, we had to relinquish our passports (for a travel permit) to the Shanghai Police. Permission was granted based upon the availability of one-way train tickets to Nanjing. At Nanjing station, we attracted quite a group of curious spectators who had never seen a laowai (foreigner). They stood as close to us as they could without touching. We stood motionless! Eventually our car arrived, and we were whisked off to the Double Gate Hotel, probably once part of the foreign concession in Nanjing.

Our hostess, Ms. Catherine Yuan, chairman for nursing for Jiangsu Province (an area about the size of France), was past retirement age, but there were no candidates for leadership replacements. She had been to the United States thirty years prior with the Rockefeller Foundation and had not spoken English since then. She would be the translator for our program. There were about fifty nurses coming for the program with no place to meet. We finally negotiated with the hotel to rent the lobby and set it up for our meeting. This was very embarrassing for the nurses but clearly demonstrated the lack of esteem held for the nursing profession at that time. However, the meeting was a success! They brought up many of the same kinds of problems that their counterparts in the United States and other countries complained of, but they had the added limitations of government constraints. After the meeting, we were treated to a pleasant dinner and a sightseeing tour of Nanjing. We then returned to Shanghai, where we quickly retrieved our passports.

From there, we continued on to Tientjin, where we would take time away from the tour to meet with the nurses of Beijing. Our "hotel" was a huge, unattractive block of a building built by the Russians. Two doctors escorted us to the train for Beijing. Our meeting in Beijing took place at the Capitol Hospital, formerly the Peking Union Medical College Hospital and the most prestigious hospital in China. The name was changed during the Cultural Revolution but has now been restored. We met the president of the Chinese Nurses' Association, Chen Cunti, and several other nursing leaders—all well beyond retirement age. We also met "Charlie," who had been a barefoot doctor during the Cultural Revolution. He was now an office assistant and in charge of our travel.

In Beijing, our presentations were divided between three special interest groups. Mine was nursing service administration. The audience consisted mainly of supervisors and head nurses. My colleagues concentrated on staff education and research. In spite of language barriers, we all felt the meetings were successful. While many of the administrative needs and problems could be improved with changes in policies and requirements, one of the most difficult ones was how to bring the level of skill of the staff up to present day standards. New staff, usually fresh out of high school, was assigned by the government with little regard for nursing interest or skills—and they were paid whether at work or not! One might compare their nursing capabilities to that of a nursing aide.

After our meetings, we were treated to dinner at the International Club. Attending were the top nursing leaders, some physicians, and government officials. One elderly and very dignified gentleman was impeccably dressed in the Mao style but with a lighter shade of blue for his suit. We learned that he had survived the "Long March" with Mao. He often attended dinners such as this to entertain and inform visitors of his great ordeal. There was also another man who seemed totally unrelated to the group. We found out that he was a "party member" keeping watch on the activities and conversation of the group. He did not speak English.

When Charlie was about to take us to the train for Tientjin, he realized he had left our tickets in the office. We were to be met in Tientjin, and the attendants would be informed to let us through "without our cancelled tickets." However, when we exited the train and tried to go on, the gates slammed down in front of us! The police were called. Of course, this created a scene and spectators soon gathered to watch the laowai (foreigners). Fortunately, our escorts finally arrived and rescued us. The remainder of our trip through China was uneventful. Each of us found the experience rewarding, and we continued our work with China in different ways. Susan later spent three months with Project Hope, teaching in the University at Xian. Kathryn has pursued other interests, and I continued to work with the Chinese Nurses' Association whenever requested.

While the Chinese could not financially sponsor travel for visiting lecturers, they often used the "side door" way of providing accommodations and meals, relying on favors owed. On several of my trips, I stayed at the Beijing Hotel, old but prestigious, diagonally across from Tiananmen Square and beside the Forbidden City. On one occasion, I arrived late at night and was given a second floor room at the front of the building. When I arose in the morning, the street was decorated with flags and banners. What a wonderful welcome, I thought, but it was really for President Reagan who was arriving that day. On two occasions, I had the rare privilege of staying with my friend, Catherine Yuan in Nanjing, but we had to register at the party office for permission.

One of my projects was to lecture in six cities on the use of computers in nursing. In my travels, I had found only two hospitals that had a computer used by hospital administration. The plan was that my friend, Dr. R. Sun (Boston University Education) would be teaching primary nursing one day and I would do my presentations the next day, giving the nurses time for sightseeing, shopping, and relaxing. The computer program was rather short. I needed to expand my presentation.

The nursing group had not yet identified care of the elderly as a potential problem. Families in China took care of their elders, but now, with the One Child per Family program, one couple could have several parents and/or grandparents to care for and still have to work. I added care of the aging to my subject matter for the lecture. The program was well received, with many doctors also in attendance, especially in Shanghai. When I talked about care of the aging patient, the audience laughed at the thought of daycare and was sure I was just making it up. To them, daycare was for babies and young children only. The impact of "one child" would soon be a reality.

The most rewarding aspect of this program was that I traveled from one place to another with the new president of the Chinese Nurses' Association, Madam Lin, and a few other nursing leaders. We enjoyed some laughs and relaxation but spent most of the time discussing nursing problems and potential solutions. I wondered if I would ever hear that some of these recommendations had been accomplished.

Sometime later, I was asked by the president of the Beijing Medical Association to do a presentation on infection control and hand washing. I contacted one of the major pharmaceutical companies in the United States regarding any interest in the program. They responded by sending two representatives (one a Chinese from Hong Kong) and a supply of samples. We would do the presentation in five hospitals in Beijing. At first I was excited to have a Chinese involved, but I soon learned that he did not speak Mandarin Chinese (only Cantonese), so his input was by demonstration only. My audience spoke Mandarin, the official dialect of China.

It was easy to see why there were problems with infection control, and improved hand washing would only solve part of the problems. Beijing is very hot and dusty in the summertime. The buildings were not air-conditioned. Many of the hospital windows were kept open and without screens. The impact of the program was limited until the larger scope of the problem, although recognized, was corrected.

Life and work in China, like every place else, had its good and bad times. In the mid 1980s, it seemed as though anyone who had a skill and could say hello in English wanted to find a way to be sponsored to the United States. I was visiting an industrial town near Tientjin. There were three restaurants, and the chefs hoped that I could find a way to sponsor them. They decided to prepare a banquet with their top entrées for me to sample. In return, I was to make something sweet. Once lunch was over, the restaurant kitchen was mine. My daughter was with me, and we looked for potential ingredients. I found cocoa, sugar (very coarse), butter, vanilla, eggs (very small!), and flour. With luck and adjusting the ingredients, I made brownies and topped them with pine nuts. The chefs thought the brownies were fine, but my daughter and I really had the better part of the deal! However, I do not know of any other Western nurse being invited to make a delicacy in a Chinese restaurant in China!

In 1989, I was scheduled to go to Beijing for the Medinfo '89 conference. Because of the Tiananmen Square tragedy, the conference was split, with part held in Singapore. Beijing was in difficult times. I needed to do some research at the Museum of History, just off Tiananmen Square. Tiananmen Square was blocked off from the public, and in order to enter, I had to show my passport. Ling, a young nurse who had been my translator, was with me. At first, she was denied admission, but after showing her identification, she was allowed to enter. By that time, the museum was closed! Ling was very embarrassed to be subjected to such an ordeal. Although trying to be inconspicuous, armed guards were everywhere—the city was changed!!

1999 was the ninetieth anniversary of the Chinese Nurses' Association. Madam Lin, who had been president of the association most of the twenty years I had been involved, sent me a special invitation to the celebration. This visit, I was the guest of a Dr. Wu, a delightful elderly cardiac surgeon. In the 1930s and 1940s, he had been at the Peter Bent Brigham Hospital with Dr. Elliot Cutler, working on new aspects of cardiac surgery. Dr. R. Sun and Ms. Yuan were also planning to attend. The conference was held in a lovely new hotel in Beijing with a large auditorium—and lunch was provided. This was quite a change from my first experience in Nanjing.

Madam Lin's presentation, summing up the past twenty years of her career, was a slide show in which she individually honored each of the nurses who had contributed to the modernization and improvement of nursing in China. It was most humbling and rewarding to stand when called and see my photo on screen with some of the nurses I had met during those years. After the program, Dr. Sun, Ms. Yuan, and I had lunch with several of the nurses we had worked with. One was now a gerontology nurse, and two others gave me copies of their research work. In nursing education, there are several new baccalaureate and masters programs. Now, relative education and competence are part of the criteria considered for professional advancement, as Chinese nursing strives toward excellence in contemporary nursing practice. What a change twenty years can bring about!

There are personal satisfactions and remembrances for me as an individual. China has changed. I miss the sight of a mass of blue- or gray-jacketed forms riding ahead on their bicycles. Now the roads are clogged with cars. I miss being able to go out late afternoon or early morning and walk in the shadow of the ancient walls of a city or in the shade of plane (sycamore) trees guarding the way. Everyone is scurrying to the bus or car. I miss walking in the alleys through the *hutongs* (neighborhoods), catching a glimpse of private life. I will miss the music—sometimes light and enchanting and other times somewhat melancholy and haunting—played on ancient stringed or wind instruments. I delight in having known a wonderful ninety-year-old Chinese-American lady, Eva, who returned to China to establish a Chinese Opera School for children. She hopes that this ancient style of song and acting will live on. I miss my dear friend Catherine Yuan, now retired from the profession she loved and a role model for all. And it was impressive to visit the Peking Union Medical College Hospital again and see the complete renovation of the interior of the ambulatory unit—comparable to the best in the United States.

China has changed, and I am thankful that I had the opportunity to experience it while it was still sleepy and then watch life improve for many and (in the big cities) take off as if propelled by some outer force. However, the lone farmer can still be seen tending his rice paddies, and the beauty of the sunset over the Suchow canals is timeless. I was fortunate to have been in the right place at the right time for the beginning of this journey. I harbor a bit of pride in the thought that I might have been a small stimulus for change, and I rejoice in knowing that nursing will meet the challenge. Twenty years, what an amazing journey!

Fore, She Said

Dorothy Gilman

I love the game of golf and played for more than thirty years at the beautiful Thorny Lea golf course in Brockton, Massachusetts. My husband, being a very good golfer and a very patient man, taught me the game, and, in time, I became a fairly good golfer. In 1989, I was lucky enough to become club champion at Thorny Lea.

Then one day, at the age of seventy-five, I stood at the tee at the par three third hole—138 yards—which I had played so many times before and swung my trusty five wood. Lo and behold, the ball disappeared into the cup! It was a hole in one! A golfer's dream come true, and it was mine!

I ran down to the green and looked into the cup. Yes, it was really there! I picked the ball up and held it high, did a little dance, and waved to the group I was playing with.

Although I can no longer play the game, I have replayed that hole in one in my mind many, many times!

I am still glued to the TV set whenever they're showing a golf tournament, and the following poem soon became my husband's favorite.

<u>My Wife Is a Golfer</u>

My wife is a golfer. She's pretty far gone.
She spiked up the carpet and hacked up the lawn.
She once won a golf ball, by default to be sure.
Now she's getting ready to make the pro tour.
She's given up ironing; my shirts are drip-dry.
When buttons are missing, she glues on a tie.
I've learned to drink breakfast, that quick instant slime,
And thaw out my dinner at tournament time.
We've adjusted our love life since she took up golf.
She's deaf to that sweet talk when her putting is off.
But fellows, remember—and have no remorse—
She can't spend your money
When she's out on the course.
(author unknown)

East Anglia

Roy D. Larson

After being on deferment (government work), my friend Herb and I enlisted into the air force. Herb went into the Signal Corps and I went into Armament. From Camp Devens to the hotel on the Boardwalk in Atlantic City. Then to Lowry Field in Denver for school. We learned about bombs and had to dismantle a fifty-caliber machine gun and put it back in its original form while blindfolded!

We were assigned to the 385th Bomb Group at Geiger Field in Spokane, Washington. From there we went to Great Falls, Montana, in April of 1943. I was in the 548th Bomb Squad, and we sailed on the *Queen Mary* in June of 1943. There were twelve bunks in the stateroom. Every other night we slept in the room and on the deck with our two barrack bags. It took us a week with no convoy to zigzag across the Atlantic to Gourac, Scotland. We took a train to Great Ashfield Airbase in East Anglia. Two planes in our squadron were lost flying over. We lived in a metal Nissan hut. We usually would load bombs at night. If the weather changed (it usually did), we would have to go back and unload and put in practice bombs. We would wait in the field for the planes to return. The ambulances would be there for the injured airmen. Very few of our original flyers survived.

Before dawn on May 22, 1944, an intruding JU88 dropped seven bombs on our base. One bomb hit a hangar and set fire to "Powerful Katrina," making it the only occasion on record when the Luftwaffe had destroyed a B-17 at its base. We also heard very noisy unmanned buzz bombs pass nearby on their way to London.

My older brother, Mike, enlisted in the Air Corps before me. He became a B-24 pilot and his 445th bomb group landed near Norwich Thorpe in East Anglia in October 1943. Jimmy Stewart was in his group but in another squadron. My friend

Dick and I found out where the base was and were able to visit him there. His crew asked a lot of questions about our flying crews and how many were killed and MIA. We could not tell them only a few were left. Fortunately, they flew twenty-nine missions and lost no one. We spent the night there and went for breakfast at the same place Jimmy Stewart was having his.

Mike and I got together a few times, and he went back to the states. President Roosevelt died, and Mike was piloting a B-24 flying over the funeral. His crew always contacted one another on New Year's Day. Mike died in 2005 when he was eighty-eight years old.

They asked for volunteers from our group to be waist gunners. One volunteered. On his second mission, they were on oxygen and hit by flak. The radioman needed help, and the waist gunner threw off his oxygen mask to help; the others didn't notice until it was too late.

The Dutch population was reduced to starvation from flooded countrysides and disrupted communication. The allies arranged with the Germans through neutral sources for food supplies to be dropped from the air. The first day 396 B-17s unloaded over seven hundred tons of rations at two airfields and a racetrack at The Hague and at an open space near Rotterdam. They did this for the next six days, and some of us were asked to go. The Dutch people scrambled to pick up the packages and had big signs on sheets saying "Thank you, Boys."

We went to London often and saw a lot of the sights. London Bridge, palaces, cathedrals, etc. There were balloons over London, taxicabs' headlights painted black, and the fog was very thick.

In June of 1945, some of us flew home on B-17s. Some went on the *Queen Elizabeth*. It took us a week to fly home, stopping at Iceland and Greenland and landing at Windsor Locks, Connecticut. I was sent to Alamogordo, New Mexico, for training on B-29s. The war was over in August, and I was discharged October 9th. Mary and I were married sixteen days later, and we are still together!

After we retired, we visited England with my wife's brother and wife. We found our airbase. All we saw was one runway filled with bales of hay and one Nissan hut in the woods. It was a big farm before the war and was one once again.

A Male Mentor for a Hesitant Woman

Kathleen M. Dodds

In 1961, while working in the bookkeeping department of a Boston bank, I met someone who would have a profound effect on my life. For thirty-nine years, he would be my mentor, confidant, and best friend. Jim Lordan managed the check-processing department, which interacted on a daily basis with my department. Because of our day-to-day contact, we formed a friendship. Jim would later go on to become a senior vice president responsible for the bank's operations division, and I would be promoted to an assistant vice president in charge of the Corporate Cash Management area. Throughout my career, he would take the time to guide and encourage me. He seemed to sense when self-doubt set in.

One specific incident comes to mind. I was offered a significant promotion and refused it, believing I did not have the right qualifications to do the job. Jim, knowing this, arranged for me to attend a conference at the American Institute for Banking. The conference was on affirmative action. One session dealt with the difference between men and women when offered upward mobility in their companies: men readily accept, thinking, "Damn the torpedoes, full speed ahead." Some women, on the other hand, practice paralysis by analysis; unfortunately, I was one of them. I left the lecture knowing that I had made a bad decision in refusing the promotion. In those days, we women were mostly less confident and less ambitious than women today a half century later.

The angels, however, were on my side. Or maybe it was just affirmative action. But the job had not been filled, and it was again offered to me. This time I accepted and so began an exciting and fulfilling career.

But there were many times in the future that I would face self-doubt, and Jim would be there as if he knew instinctively that I needed a friend. He was always there for me but would not let me depend on him, so I learned to depend on myself. He influenced me both personally and professionally. What I lacked in my life—individuality and recognition—were qualities Jim encouraged. These are now the themes in my life.

Jim guided me to achieve the control I needed over my life to make decisions, to take risks, to be both productive and creative—all of the qualities necessary to a successful career. He encouraged me to be all I could be, and for this alone, I will be eternally grateful. Jim was unique; sometimes, I think he was one of Gods angels on earth. For they walk the earth unnoticed, yet they notice all, they relate to all, see all, and know all.

I guess I am putting this on paper today because I am not sure that I said thank you while you were here to hear it. And I need to say it: thank you, Jim.

My Visit to the Philippines

John H. Arthur

When I learned that one of the memoir workshop teachers was a native of the Philippines, it brought back memories for me because I had the opportunity, while in the U.S. Army, to visit her native land many years ago. While the Philippines was not my primary destination, circumstances resulted in my spending ten days there in 1955.

While stationed on Okinawa, my friend Carl and I decided to take leave and go to Bangkok, Thailand. For enlisted personnel, military transportation was the most affordable way to get there. It required flying to either Taiwan (formerly Formosa) or to Clark Air Base in the Philippines. To travel to either country, I had to obtain a visa. So I wrote to my mom in Milton, Massachusetts, asking her to mail my birth certificate so that I could get the necessary visa.

The first flight available was scheduled to land in Taiwan and then fly on to Bangkok. Because my birth certificate did not arrive in time, however, I had to cancel this flight. Tragically, the plane I would have been on crashed into a mountain on Taiwan in bad weather, killing all on board. This is the only time I was grateful the mails were late.

Two weeks later, after getting my visa, we flew to Clark Air Base in the Philippines. We waited two days in the hope of getting on a flight to Bangkok. While waiting, we stayed at the base and relaxed. On the second day, we went to the pool. It was 105 degrees outside, and when we jumped into the pool, we were shocked; the water was ice cold, about 60 degrees. The lifeguard, a young Filipino lad, just laughed. Then we sat down and chatted with him. He told us to forget trying to get on the Bangkok embassy flight the next day. He said it was always full because a commercial plane rather than a military aircraft is used. Instead, he suggested we stay in the Philippines.

With ten days available, the lifeguard suggested we visit three places: the city of Baguio in the mountains one hundred miles from Manila where the cold water came from; Tagaytay, a city on a volcano south of Manila near Lake Taal; and the island of Corregidor in Manila Harbor. This last place, Corregidor, held memories for me. As a young boy, I followed the events of World War II and the Pacific theater after the Japanese attack on Pearl Harbor.

And so we moved from Clark Air Base to the YMCA in downtown Manila next to the Presidential Palace. From there, we visited all three of the places the young lifeguard at the base had recommended. The trip to Corregidor stands out in my memory as the most meaningful. For most Filipinos on a Sunday afternoon in 1955 it was a boat excursion, a chance to relax, play mah jong, have a picnic lunch, and enjoy friends. But for me, it was much more nostalgic.

I was ten years old in 1941. My memories of the war came from the weekly newsreels on the screen at the Oriental Theater in Mattapan. One such memory was about the courageous Americans and Filipinos on the island of Corregidor who held out from December 7, 1941, until the island surrendered on May 5, 1942. During this time, the island was under constant bombardment by the Japanese. You may remember that Gen. Douglas MacArthur left the island by PT boat before the surrender. He vowed to the people of the Philippines that he would return. To actually walk in the island's dust and see the rock caverns and the shell marks on the walls were very meaningful to me because of the sacrifice the people stationed there had made.

An incident on the return trip was a reminder of how General MacArthur was still highly revered by the Filipino people. Two WACs (Women's Army Corp) were talking in a negative manner about his conduct in the Korean War. Several angry Filipinos came forward to express how they still greatly admired him because he kept his promise in World War II to return and free the Philippines from the Japanese occupation. Were it not for the intervention of a Filipino doctor, I believe the two WACs would have been thrown overboard by the Filipinos.

After those anxious moments had passed, we talked to the doctor. Before Bataan fell to the Japanese, he had swum across the bay from Mariveles, at the southern tip of Bataan to Corregidor. When Corregidor fell in 1942, he was interned by the Japanese but later escaped. He then joined the Filipino guerillas and fought the Japanese for the remainder of the war. He was a real hero and was very grateful to all the American servicemen who had helped free his country.

We also visited the University of Santo Thomas, site of the Japanese POW camp for the survivors of the Bataan death march. It was called Camp O'Donnell and had been rebuilt after the war. At the time of my visit, it was a beautiful college campus with poinsettias lining the walkways and gardens within.

Our Filipino work associates on Okinawa also invited us to a college graduation party in Manila. While we did not know these young graduates, we were made to feel very welcome. Because we were recent college graduates from America, we spent most of the evening talking about education programs at American universities. When they learned that I was from Boston, they had more questions than I could answer about Harvard, MIT, and BU. They had never heard of Tufts University, my alma mater. It was a great evening. We enjoyed meeting these young people, and I later had the opportunity to meet one of the graduates in New York City; she had come to America for graduate studies. Her father was a member of the staff from the Philippines at the United Nations.

This was my first international trip. Later, after my return to civilian life, I had the opportunity to travel abroad and visit Alaska, Hawaii, and sixteen other countries. This enabled me to meet and work with people from different cultures during my fifty-year career as an engineer. Today, it gives me a different perspective and a better understanding than most Americans have concerning people from foreign countries and the different conditions under which they live, work, and play.

Moving to Fuller Village

Elena MacIsaac

My husband, Joe, and I were very excited to be moving to Fuller Village. On one of our advance trips, we were thrilled to find "mail" in our mailbox—the open, intra-village mailboxes across from the locked USPS mailboxes. Of course, the mail was only a copy of the Fuller Village newsletter, but it gave us a sense of belonging to Fuller Village. And the excitement grew.

As we were waiting for our appointment with a member of the Fuller Village sales team, I started to wander around the common, entering the parlor, the card room, and the café. Looking into the café, I saw a couple sitting there. Because I'm so brave, and certainly no one could accuse me of being shy, I approached the couple and asked them if they were residents. They said yes and introduced themselves as Jo and Frank Accattatis.

I asked them many questions that they didn't seem to mind, and they were very informative in their responses. They assured me that Joe and I would love living here and even told us what they preferred to eat in the café. They invited us to join them at the table, and we had our first lunch with them.

I am so grateful for their kind words, putting our minds at ease before we moved in, and we now know Fuller Village is full of people like them.

On Going to Jail and Becoming a Pioneer

Elaine Pinderhughes

It happened the summer after I graduated from college and just before I entered graduate school in 1943. I had won the coveted Lucy Moten Travel Fellowship that had enabled previous winners to travel abroad for six months. However, because of the war, I was forced to choose study and travel within the United States. I attended the Lisle Fellowship, a Quaker work camp on Lookout Mountain, Colorado, that, in itself, became a transformative experience for me.

The lectures by well-known academicians and scholars on philosophy, citizenship participation, responsibility, and spirituality came alive as we applied their principles in our weekend work deputations to the surrounding communities. We were assigned in teams to do work that met a variety of needs on farms, in churches, and in public as well as private agencies. This is where I learned of migrant farm workers. I was shocked at the squalor in which they were forced to live, and I saw the deep depression of the Japanese families who had been driven from their homes, mostly in the West, and held in internment camps. We led group recreation, taught Sunday school, and even preached sermons in these oppressed communities about which I had heard nothing back East.

The most significant experience was our participation in the annual conference of the Fellowship of Reconciliation (F.O.R.) in Denver. We helped gather data for the workshops the F.O.R. was planning on citizen action to end discrimination, and then were allowed to participate in the workshops themselves. I chose to picket a theatre known to be discriminating against Negroes and Mexicans.

After I was refused seating and the picketing began, our team was arrested. Taken in a patrol car, my watch, ring, and cash were placed in an envelope labeled with PRISONER and my name. I was separated from my team and placed in a dirty, barren cell with a bed, a small metal table, chair, and a toilet in the middle of the floor. My cellmate was a Mexican woman who said that because she had had to work, she had been arrested for child neglect. The food, which I refused to eat, was slid under the cell bars on a metal plate.

Just as I was becoming despairing and night was falling, we were released to a large crowd of supporters who were waiting outside and who cheered us.

But it was the hearing conducted to clear us picketers of charges that has remained so unforgettable to me over the years. Many citizens articulated their outrage at our arrest since Colorado had a civil rights law and we were merely calling attention to its violation. These citizens demanded that the mayor, the police department, and all of the establishments who had been violating the law cease immediately. The passion of these citizens was inspirational and astounding as were the editorials in the *Rocky Mountain News* that, ironically, just ceased publication this past year. I later learned that the gains we achieved remained until this day.

The memory of that summer dimmed as I coped with graduate school, raising five children, and launching a career as a psychiatric social worker and academician.

Occasionally, I would tell this story, and sometimes, as a joke, would shock folks with the announcement that I had a jail history.

However, the full impact of that whole experience only hit me when I was preparing to move here to Fuller. I came across the letter I had written to my then secret husband about going to the F.O.R. conference, choosing the picketing workshop, and going to jail. I shared my exhilaration at being a part of such an event, and, now safe, my fears about what my family would say about my being put in jail.

Tucked into that letter and carefully preserved was the program of that Fellowship of Reconciliation conference. It was billed as a *Workshop in Non-Violent Political Action*, something I had completely forgotten. As we know, The Fellowship of Reconciliation was the forerunner of CORE, (Congress for Racial Equality), one of the organizations that assisted Martin Luther King Jr. and his advisors, supplying philosophy, mission, manpower, and funds for the movement they led.

I realized in that moment that, in participating in that picketing workshop, in being arrested and held in jail so long ago, I had been among the first sit-inners, the early activists on the civil rights scene. I had actually been in the vanguard of the most important movement for civil rights in the history of our country!

(Top L to R) Arthur Erwin, Elaine Pinderhughes
Alan Klein
(Seated) Josephine Ferruggio, John Hemenway
Marjorie Seery

The Day Fate Served Me an Ace

Milt Glassman

How different our life's journey might have been had we taken a left turn rather than a right. I am a fatalist as well as a pragmatic realist. This is an experience when fate and destiny influenced my life.

It was the most perfect spring morning that I can remember—not a cloud in the sky, bright sun, and perfect temperature. It was 1948. I had completed a short tour in the navy and finished my pre-dental studies, receiving a BS in biology. The competition to gain admission to medical and dental school was very keen. I decided that I would spend time working before applying to dental school, allowing me to gain positive experience and earn the much-needed funds for tuition.

I was having a very difficult time locating the position to meet my needs, and job-hunting every day had become stressful and frustrating. When I awoke and saw the beautiful day, I decided to forgo my search and spend the day playing tennis.

Lo and behold, as I walked onto the court, there was a college acquaintance. We exchanged greetings and brought our experiences up to date. He told me that he was to be married to a classmate of mine in two weeks, and that she was leaving her position as a lab assistant at the Beth Israel Hospital where she worked for the pathologist in chief.

I thanked him profusely for the information, went directly home, changed into my "I-mean-business" clothes, and proceeded to the Beth Israel.

I fortunately was able to make contact with Dr. Monroe Schlesinger, who was in need of a lab assistant for his research project. After an extensive review of my resume and a lengthy interview, he welcomed me aboard. Thus began one of the most important journeys of my life. Dr. Schlesinger was the most remarkable person I have had the privilege to know. He was a pure scientist with a brilliant mind, a humble and caring human being, a teacher par excellence, and the best mentor anyone could have.

I worked with Dr. Schlesinger studying anastomotic circulation in the heart. We perfected a radiopaque mass with which the autopsied heart was perfused. This mass became an irreversible gel, red for the right tree and blue for the left. The heart was then X-rayed, and, by dissection, it was found that in many cases new circulation bypassed the damaged area of the heart and provided healthy circulation. These findings were the basis for bypass surgery that came many years later.

After two years of work on this study, Dr. Schlesinger strongly suggested that I was ready to go on and pursue my professional education. Following a call by Dr. Schlesinger to the dean of admissions of Tufts University School of Dental Medicine, I was called for an interview. After that interview was completed, I was informed that I would be welcomed as a member of the next class.

My love of tennis never diminished, and each time I walk onto a court, I remember that beautiful, fateful day when the door was opened to my career that I loved and for which I am most grateful.

The PT Boats and Solomon Islands, 1942–44

Henry Hanley

Upon graduating from Boston English High Class of 1941 and shortly after my eighteenth birthday, I volunteered for the navy and was sworn in at Post Office Square on December 7, 1942, the first anniversary of Pearl Harbor. Immediately after the swearing in, we were marched to South Station and boarded a train for the Great Lakes Naval Training Station in Green Bay, Wisconsin. Upon completion of our basic training, we were allowed a short leave home, after which I was given orders to report to radar training school in Virginia Beach, Virginia.

After completing radar training, I was ordered to report to the PT (Patrol Torpedo) boat training base in Melville, Rhode Island, and assigned to Squadron 11 (Ron 11). Subsequently, our squadron was transported to the Brooklyn Navy Yard, where our boats were to be placed into cradles on a tanker deck and taken to the Panama Canal. Upon arriving at Panama Canal, we made our way through the docks and emerged on the Pacific side. We arrived at a base where we trained and adjusted to the heat. After this, our boats were once again loaded onto the deck of a tanker, and we sailed for the Solomon Islands. We arrived in the New Hebrides Islands, a French possession, and unloaded there. From the harbor of Noumea, we made our run up to Espiritu Santo, our main navy base at that time, and then to Tulagi Island, part of the Solomon chain and adjacent to Guadalcanal.

We were apprehensive about the latter run because, due to some confusion and poor intelligence, another squadron (Ron 10) had been fired upon by our own planes. Fortunately, we made the run with no such incident. As an aside, Ron 10 had the distinction of having then Lt. John F. Kennedy as one of its PT boat skippers. Upon arriving in Tulagi, and to lighten the boat, we had to store everything that wasn't essential.

Consequently, all clothing and other items were moved to a base storeroom; we never saw them again.

From Tulagi, we went up to Rendova Island, adjacent to New Georgia Island, upon which we had a new airstrip called Munda. Joe Foss, the marine air ace, and Pappy Boyington of *Black Sheep* fame, were based there. While at Rendova, there were twelve boats from Ron 10 and six from Ron 11; six of our boats were sent to the Samoa Islands. While at Rendova, Ron 10 and Ron 11 were expected to alternate nights for patrols. When on patrol, our speed was much reduced unless we had to take evasive action due to a problem with "float" planes, Japanese aircraft that would drop flares to illuminate our presence and enable Japanese shore batteries to fire on us.

The Pacific Ocean around the islands posed two problems for our boats: 1.) The sea is very phosphorous, enabling planes to pick up our wake and pinpoint our whereabouts, and 2.) The presence of coconut logs that fall into the sea, become waterlogged and float just slightly below the surface. When returning to base from one patrol, we hit one such coconut log that punctured the bottom of the boat, creating a large hole and causing flooding of the boat. We had self-bailers that worked well if you were at great speed. But when you take in more water than you discharge, the boat loses speed, and the bailers become less effective. Fortunately, the PT boats had compartmental seals, and I was ordered to go below and see if I could locate and seal the damaged compartment; luck was with us, and I managed to do so. Otherwise, it's likely we would have been stranded in Japanese-held territory much like JFK and his crew were.

On one patrol, we had information from our base that the night before, one of Ron 10's boats failed to return due to enemy action the previous night. The skipper told us to be on the lookout for any signs of this boat. Unfortunately, we did not see it or any of its crew or their signals; the float planes (more than one) were out that night, and we had a very busy night evading the Japanese artillery. Many years later, at the JFK Presidential Library and Museum, I viewed the coconut bearing the message JFK wrote and set afloat in his effort to get our attention.

The PT boats had a crew of ten men and two officers. Every man was trained to perform necessary duties of any other including officers. The reason was obvious: to enable the boat to be functional in case of injuries to other crewmembers. When on patrol during the long night, and except for a general quarters (combat), we would have two hours on alert and one to rest. PT boats performed other duties, including picking up and dropping off "beach watchers," usually Australians who were coconut plantation overseers. We also had lots of calls to rescue downed pilots. The sea was very rough in this area and the "crash" boats normally assigned for this purpose were unable to get out and do these rescues. We were also called upon to rescue Geisha girls who were left behind by the Japanese when they abandoned an island.

The PT boats were the smallest commissioned vessels in the U.S. Navy. We had four torpedoes, two "twin" 50-caliber machine guns, one 20mm single, a 60mm mortar, a 37mm cannon movable on a tripod, and one depth charge that was very helpful in convincing Japanese who were in the water to come on board and surrender. This was especially useful at Bougainville Island. The Japanese at the end tried to evacuate their troops. Intelligence became aware of their plan, and our big ships from Espiritu Santo, including my brother's cruiser, were brought up. During this battle, we were assigned to prevent the Japanese from circling around to assault our big ships. I later learned my brother's cruiser, the USS *Denver*, was hit by an aircraft-launched torpedo but survived. The next morning we were assigned to patrol and pick up any Japanese surrenders, especially those who were in the water. Some refused to surrender, forcing us to deal with them harshly; if they were able to return to shore, they would have posed a danger to our troop movements.

PT boats had three engines with three propellers, enabling it to be very maneuverable. Reverse one propeller and leave its opposite in regular, and the boat would easily turn. Running on open seas, the PT boats were really bouncy. Seas have different lengths between crests; if the crest were less than eighty feet apart, we were able to ride from crest to crest and avoid crashing into the trough, action that caused seasickness. We had no means of obtaining fresh water except to get it externally; usually we would catch rainwater (the best) and also shower with saltwater soap while the rain lasted, or from LST's or our base. Base water was terrible and heavily chlorinated. Food was always a problem, especially fresh fruit or vegetables. When I returned from the Pacific, I only weighed

130 pounds, and I had put on some of that weight while I was being transported back aboard a Kaiser aircraft carrier. They had good food.

I recall one particular event when we were operating from the Island of Emiru. There was an unspoken disagreement between the marines and the PT boaters as to who had the toughest duty. And on occasion, we would take persons who desired to experience a patrol. Joe Foss and his group were there at the time, and some wanted to go on a patrol. They came aboard with full regalia of knives, pistols, etc., while we were dressed in shorts and shoes cut like sandals. The sandal effect kept seawater from being trapped in our shoes. On this particular run, I had to stay below deck and operate the radar; it was an excellent tool for positioning our boat the desired distance from shore, and for locating bays, inlets, etc.

When I finally was relieved, it was dark, and we were running at reduced speed. None of Foss's pilots were standing near the "Con" but were lying down on the deck instead, somewhat obstructing the passageway. The skipper asked me to try to get them up and out of the way. On the boat, we had four aerial torpedoes that were merely allowed to roll off at launching. However, the sea regularly washed over them, and it was important to protect them from the saltwater. What we did was coat the warheads with heavy grease. Alas, I had to lash three of Foss's pilots to three of the torpedoes because they were so seasick, they could easily have washed overboard. When we returned, the pilots were so anxious to go ashore, they leapt from the boat while we were still docking; they departed with no good-byes or other pleasantries.

My boat, MTB178, was a lucky boat. We lost only one shipmate, and that was due to a gas leak that filled the bilges and caught on fire. The PT boats were equipped with a CO2 system that could be activated from the "Con." This was done, and the fire was extinguished, saving the boat and all but one crewmember, Van, who was on duty in the engine room and was burned to death. I'll never forget him and the other brave sailors and marines who lost their lives. Australia was saved and perhaps even the United States by their sacrifices. May they rest in peace and never be forgotten.

On my final day, the boat's colors (flag and pennants) were changed; the wind and sea were hard on them, and they were regularly replaced. The skipper gave me our boat's retired colors, and I have kept them to this day. I returned to the United States a very lucky sailor who survived. I learned later my squadron was transferred to the Philippines, along with General MacArthur, and was actively engaged in the decisive defeat of the Japanese fleet there.

A Navy "Well done," Ron 11; shipmates forever!

Veterans Day

J. Alexander Harte

For more than thirty-five years, I was the American Legion contact for Memorial Day and Veterans Day programs in the Town of Milton. During the eight years preceding my retirement, I was in full charge of both programs. At some point, I realized something was missing at the town hall: a memorial commemorating the local veterans who died in the service of our nation.

Thinking about this, I initiated a plan with the legion to donate a fitting memorial. With the legion's approval, we met with the town selectmen. They agreed it was an excellent idea and gave their approval for us to go forward with the project at our discretion.

The next hurdle was to find a suitable location for the memorial. The only area that provided enough space was a wall inside the town hall. The selectmen relocated a memorial clock that had been displayed on that wall, thereby freeing the wall for our use. After agreeing upon the location, we began work on the project.

Many hours were spent compiling, via town records and other sources, the names that would be displayed on the memorial. When completed, the list was forwarded to a bronze foundry where the names would be forged or cast onto four separate plaques.

After discussions with the foundry regarding the design and cost of the four plaques, we ordered them to be manufactured. The plaques were for World War I, World War II, the Korean conflict, and the Vietnam conflicts. Together, they contain the names of 124 individuals who died in the service of our country: 26 in World War I, 87 in World War II, 6 in Korea, and 5 in Vietnam.

When the plaques arrived, we then designed a suitable mounting board. Mounted on the board were the four bronze plaques, the five service emblems, and a separate bronze plaque stating: THEY MADE THE SUPREME SACRIFICE.

I had the pleasure of dedicating the Veterans Memorial and donating it to the Town of Milton from American Legion Post #114 on Veterans Day, November 11, 1996. The memorial is now located inside the town hall entrance for all to see.

(Top L to R) Milton and Blossom Glassman
Mae Evangelista, Jack McCarthy
(Seated) Catherine Gilligan, Eugene Panarese
Dorothy Gilman

Walking with My Dad

Thomas O'Connor

My father was a mailman, a quiet, serious man who loved his job and enjoyed all the people he met. On the one hand, he was very strict about obeying rules and regulations and insisted on treating all people with the respect they deserved regardless of their race or religion. On the other hand, he had a wonderful sense of humor and enjoyed music of all sorts.

Perhaps because he was a letter carrier, my father liked to walk. Fortunately, at the age of ten, I was old enough to enjoy walking with him. Occasionally, after school, my mother would let me walk down to the South Boston Post Office on West Broadway to meet my father when his route was over. Usually, I would have to sit quietly off to the side while my father and several other letter carriers sorted out their deliveries for the next day, distributing envelopes into the proper slots with unerring accuracy. When the work was completed, I would walk along Broadway with my father, greeting all kinds of people along the way who recognized him in his blue uniform.

On Sunday afternoons in the winter months, we would walk up to M Street Park to watch football games. During the 1930s and 1940s, before professional football leagues made their appearance, most Knights of Columbus chapters in the Greater Boston area fielded first-rate semi-pro football teams made up largely of former football stars from such colleges as Boston College, Holy Cross, Fordham, Georgetown, and Villanova, who were keeping in shape. After the game, my dad and I would walk back home where my mother always had a hot supper waiting.

During the summer months, after he came home from work, my father would take us up to M Street Park to watch baseball games. During the twenties, former New England League pitcher, Bill "Twilight" Kelly, promoted semi-pro baseball games on Saturday and Sunday afternoons during the twilight hours. Working men could get home from work in the afternoon, gulp down a quick bite, and then enjoy six or seven innings of baseball before darkness closed in. "Twilight" brought in some of the best semi-pro teams in the country—including the Harlem Colored All Stars from New York, and the heavily bearded House of David team from Salt Lake City. Between innings, "Twilight" would make his way through the bleachers with a big tin dipper, collecting enough money to buy beer for the players after the game.

Some of my favorite walks came on those Sunday afternoons when we decided to go to the movies. Dad and I would walk down L Street, cross the Summer Street Bridge, and then continue along Summer Street to Washington Street to the Loew's Orpheum Theater. During the Depression years, Loew's put on live vaudeville shows during their Sunday matinees, followed by the main attraction. Sometimes it would be a gangster movie with James Cagney and Pat O'Brien. Other times it might be a lively musical with Dick Powell, Ruby Keeler, and a colorful Busby Berkeley production.

Movies were always fun for the both of us, but on one occasion the atmosphere was different when we attended a showing of *All Quiet on the Western Front.* That afternoon, my father was strangely quiet as we sat there together and watched the bloody slaughter of trench warfare on the battlefields of World War I. And on the walk home, instead of the usual conversations we had about how good the movie was and what actors we liked best, my father just made a few casual remarks but said little about the motion picture itself.

It was only later, shortly after my father had died, that I began to appreciate the reason for his silence that day. I knew that he had been a member of the 42nd ("Rainbow") Division in World War I and that he had served overseas. Beyond that, however, he had never spoken about his wartime experiences. Going through his bureau drawer later, I found a small tin box with a rusted German belt buckle, along with several medals and campaign bars indicating that he had fought in the Battle of St. Mihiel and the Argonne Forest. Along with these, I found a copy of his discharge papers, indicating that he had been gassed and had also been wounded by a trench knife.

Walking with my dad, I had found out many things about his likes and his dislikes (he hated any man wearing his hat in the house), his interests and his skills (he was a fine carpenter), and his beliefs and his convictions (he was convinced you could be anything you wanted to be). But there were obviously some things he kept to himself and didn't want anyone else to know. Perhaps that's the way things should be. Maybe parents would prefer to shield their children from painful reminders of the past. Who knows?

The O'Donnell Farm in Washington, NH

Patricia Bray

I was a teenager when my father bought the house in Washington, New Hampshire. It was a perfect vacation home for my parents and their eleven children.

How I loved going up there on weekends, and especially on summer vacations. It was a beautiful place to be at any time of year, even in winter! I have so many stories to share, but I want to describe a typical weekend there.

On Friday night, we would all drive up to Washington for our weekend stay. As soon as we arrived, we would jump out of the car to see how many porcupines we could find. There were so many of them, they were a nuisance for everyone. They would bite into car tires, flattening them. They would get into houses, ours as well, and cause damage. There was a bounty on them, and we would bring them to the town hall where we would get fifty cents for each one.

Mother was in charge of the oil lamps. We had no electricity or running water. There was a pump at the back door. Water would be put into a big kettle that would be placed on the back of a big black stove to heat up so that we would have hot water for all our needs. We did not have the luxury of indoor plumbing, but we did have "Outhouse #5." When we visited it at night, the dew on the grass was so wet that our shoes and socks would be completely soaked. Animals would scamper around us, scaring us as we made our way to and from the house in the dark.

On Saturday night, we would go through the woods to the square dance in Bradford. The ride was beautiful, and we could see deer in the fields as we drove along. Square dancing was always so much fun and certainly tired us out! Coming home, we could see all the oil lamps glowing in the windows. They filled us with such a warm feeling. Father would have the fireplace going and would have hot dogs and hamburgers with all the fixings for us to eat.

We had so many good times. In winter, we went skiing at Sunapee. We would leave our car at the bottom of the hill and drag our sled, filled with skis, up the slopes for a great day of skiing. In summer, we spent lazy days swimming and boating in the Ashuelot River Lake near our home.

On Sunday morning, my mother would make a big breakfast of bacon and eggs with her famous blueberry muffins, and then off we would go to church. In winter, we often went by toboggan when snow closed the roads.

We always brought friends with us, and many times our house would be filled with twenty people. On Sundays, my uncle and his sisters would come from Manchester. Sunday dinner was always out on the front lawn, and Uncle Joe would bring balloons for all of us—very festive! My mother did all the cooking, and all the kids did the cleanup. The dishes were washed out in the backyard on a table next to the well. It was teamwork: some would bring the dirty dishes to the wash site, some would wash, some would dry, and others would put everything away.

When the time came to leave, we would all help get the house in order and then return home with new stories to share and happy times to remember.

America the Beautiful

John Dooley

This memoir recounts a 1973 trip to Czechoslovakia, Russia, Ukraine, and Germany with the New England Sports Ambassadors All-Star Hockey Team.

The team was composed of boys between the ages of sixteen and eighteen, mostly from the Greater Boston area. I was extremely proud when my captain, Joe Rando, was selected for the team. He, as well as all the other players, quickly became molded into a tremendous hockey team. Coaches Tim Taylor and Gene Kinasawich accomplished the difficult task of selecting and preparing the team.

Before leaving on the journey, we attended many preparatory meetings at Harvard. Aside from presenting general information, seminars were conducted on the political, cultural, geographic, and economic composition of the various countries. Films, historians, and guest speakers provided us with new insights and background regarding the mysteries that lay behind the Iron Curtain. The question and answer period that occurred during these meetings gave me the feeling that even if we never got off the ground, we had received a tremendous course in Eastern European History.

After a long flight with stopovers in Ireland and Germany, we arrived in Prague, the capital of Czechoslovakia. The initial feeling upon arriving and penetrating an Iron Curtain country was one of anxiety and even fear. My own excitement was generated from two sources. First, being a history major, I could finally associate much of my studies with firsthand views of these textbook places. Secondly, being a hockey coach, I would have the opportunity to see and learn the new revolutionary style of Eastern European hockey.

Our visit to Czechoslovakia was the most meaningful, mainly because we were there for six days and had the opportunity to become familiar with the people and the country—

especially the city of Prague. Small, winding cobblestone streets, ancient buildings, and small shops helped to create the antiquity of the city. Old-fashioned trolley cars, along with modern buses, provided the majority of the people with transportation that operated on the honor system for fares.

The people, in spite of being dominated by the Soviet Union, still maintained strong nationalistic feelings. However, they lacked the industrious vigor that characterizes Americans. This is perhaps due to the economic control of business and industry by the state that subdued incentive. The Czechs had a tremendous dislike for the Russians. During a conversation with one of the Czech coaches, I asked him about the possibility of bringing his team to the United States, and he said it was impossible because "we are Russian puppets." Also, during a conversation with the hotel manager, he talked about the good old days, inferring that these were bad times.

The outlying areas of Czechoslovakia reminded one of the flat farm regions of Kansas and North Dakota. Scattered along the way were stucco villages completely enclosed by walls that housed the communal cooperative families, animals, and machinery.

The rinks, for the most part, were modern and not only oversized in playing surface but also in total structure. The boys won two and lost two to the Czechs. One of the teams that beat us was recognized as the second best team in the country. This team, Dukla—an army team—gave a clinic after the game displaying some of their drills. The one that interested me the most was one that started as a 5–0 with the furthermost player turning as a defenseman and creating a 4–1. This was repeated going the other way, thus allowing one of the other players the experience as a defenseman. In general, their drills represented precision passing and continuous motion.

Before each game, the boys exchanged gifts with the opponents; and after the games, we were hosted to banquets. It was during these occasions that the boys developed a closer understanding and appreciation toward their Czech counterparts. This was all accomplished in spite of the language barrier. Also, one can appreciate the extreme difficulties faced by the immigrants to the United States and the necessity of settling into ethnic neighborhoods.

Perhaps the most fearful sight in Czechoslovakia was the presence of Russian tanks and soldiers. We saw them upon returning from a three-hour trip from Jihlava in the darkness of night. We were stopped at a railroad crossing on a deserted road, and on the other side was a Russian convoy. Needless to say, a concerned silence engulfed the bus. Up to this point, I'm sure none of us really realized the significance of living in a communist-dominated country.

From Czechoslovakia, we went to Moscow to embark on a sleeper train to Kiev in the Ukraine. While waiting at the railroad station, which was right out of a World War II movie, I felt very uncomfortable. The station was quite busy, and the air was filled with the odor of damp coal. Soldiers and police milled about as people hurried by carrying immense loads. Old women carried blankets full of goods on their backs, and both hands were occupied toting heavy bags. Evidently, they bring their goods to the city and sell them, then carry supplies back to the village. While we were in the station, the doctor who was with our party was taken into a room and interrogated. It was just a routine check, but the doctor seemed a bit pale after the experience. Along our twelve-hour train excursion from Moscow to Kiev, we passed barren, frozen wasteland.

We toured Kiev, a city that offered a blending of the new and old. There seemed to be construction everywhere, and most of the vehicles in the streets were trucks. The city, like Prague, was exceptionally clean. Women with brooms and shovels were constantly sweeping the sidewalks. Giant-sized posters of Lenin and the symbol of the hammer and sickle became more obvious.

I was amazed that a great deal of nationalism still pervaded among the Ukrainians despite the fact that it was one of the Soviet states. One evening we had the opportunity to eat at a Ukrainian restaurant, which boasted a fifteen-course dinner. While there, a large Ukrainian family having a reunion sat behind us and began singing an old folk song. They were told to stop, and an uneasy quiet settled on the room. Once again, the concept of freedom faded away.

Athletics in these countries were controlled by area clubs and subsidized by the state. The clubs were situated in beautiful stadiums and sport complexes. Each sport had its own identity and was centrally controlled. As an athlete moves up the ladder from a basic team to an all-star team, his training became more scientific and structured.

Most of the top athletes are enrolled in the Sports Institute and received year-round training. Because they were subsidized, and participation in athletics was their prime function, they were professionals. The top athletes went to Moscow where they participate on the National Team and prepare for the Olympics.

From Kiev, we again went on the twelve-hour train excursion to Moscow. The city itself was bulging at the seams with people, as there were seven million inhabitants and two million transients. Apartment after apartment gave the city the appearance of being nothing but apartment complexes. However, it was pointed out that one half of all the goods produced in the Soviet Union came from Moscow. The Kremlin and Red Square were very impressive sights, mainly because of the historical background they represent. Scattered throughout the city were beautiful golden-onion-domed cathedrals. They are maintained purely for aesthetic purposes, as religion was practically non-existent in the Iron Curtain countries.

Moscow, like many of our cities, reflected a melting pot, with the exception of blacks. The people appeared very mechanical and unemotional. They seem to like the fun and frolicking nature that we possessed. I'm sure this was a result of many years of hard times resulting from wars and revolution as well as their earlier suppression by the czars.

The Russians boasted of many great social benefits such as free education and medical services, retirement based on 75 percent of one's income, rents of 5 percent of income, and they expected to provide free gas and electricity by 1975.

The people in Moscow were well dressed and appeared well fed. However, I, for one, am not a fan of Russian food.

The underground subways were immaculate with shiny white walls and highly decorative chandeliers hanging from the ceilings.

While in Moscow, I had the opportunity to see the opening of the World Hockey Games with Russia playing West Germany. They were held in the beautiful arena where the Canada-Russia series was played.

From Moscow, we went to West Berlin by way of East Berlin. The contrast was like night and day. West Berlin is very modern. However, in the reconstruction of the city, much of the German architecture and traditional décor was preserved. Many single-family houses and townhouses with lawns and gardens exist. East Berlin still had some of the rubble from World War II, and bombed out buildings were still in evidence. The city, in spite of new construction, still appeared drab and without life.

Perhaps the most frightening sight of the entire trip was the gaudy appearance of the Berlin Wall. Positioned along the wall were towers with armed guards. Pacing between the walls were vicious German Shepherds. Every week, successful and unsuccessful escape attempts were made. We were told that three Russian soldiers were recently shot while trying to defect.

The most eye-catching sight for me during the trip was the variety of jobs I saw women performing. For example, I saw women carpenters, masons, laborers, truck drivers, railroad workers, farmers—every job a man did, a woman did. They must have been liberated.

The trip can be evaluated in many ways. Certainly it was great to watch one of my players, Joe Rando, play fine hockey and show the Russians what body checking is all about. Representing the Massachusetts hockey coaches and observing Eastern European hockey at firsthand afforded the opportunity of a lifetime for a hockey coach. But perhaps the most significant value of the tour for me as well as for the entire group was a deeper appreciation of the United States. All too often we take for granted our simple freedoms. I'm grateful that I live in a country where my mail isn't inspected, where I can move about at my own pleasure, where I can choose my own station in life, and where I can practice my own belief in God.

As our plane approached the runway at Logan Airport, I overheard a couple of the boys humming "America the Beautiful," hence the title of this memoir. This spontaneous action by the boys proved to me the value of the trip.

In closing, the success of this trip was the direct result of the tireless efforts of the co-directors, Tim Taylor and Gene Kinasawich. During the tour, both Tim and Gene gave unselfishly of themselves to insure that everyone received a totally rewarding experience. I know that this was achieved and that every member of the group is extremely grateful to these men for their efforts.

GOD BLESS AMERICA!

Nice ‘n Easy Number 60

Agnes Walker

Several years ago, when I was in my early seventies, my son, then in his late thirties, stopped by to visit. He was looking down on my head and commented that my hair roots were showing white; he asked why I had not “touched up” my hair.

Kiddingly, I explained that I was letting it grow out to show how old I really was and then my children, now adults, would expect less of me! He quite seriously said that he did not want to see me with white hair and asked, “What’s the name of that stuff you use?” I told him, in jest, “Nice ‘n Easy Number 60.”

This month, my daughter, age fifty, arrived at her office with a different hair color. One of her associates suggested that she let nature take its course, but she responded, “I refuse to go gray before my mom.”

It is my intent that my son, sadly who is no longer with us, shall never see my hair go “white.”

A Doctor's Education

Tom White

After medical school at Emory University and an internship in Boston, I went to New Orleans for a pediatric residency at Charity Hospital. "Big" Charity in New Orleans and six small satellite hospitals scattered around Louisiana had been built in the 1930s by Huey Long, the demagogic governor. He was a huge thorn in FDR's side with his slogan: "Every Man a King." He told the poor people of Louisiana (which was most of them) to come to Charity whenever they got sick, and all the care was free. The medical services were run by the medical schools of Tulane University and Louisiana State University. So everybody won! Resident doctors received superb training and got to see nearly every disease known. The poor were taken care of—albeit with the possible disadvantages of being treated by doctors still in training.

The first year of pediatric training was at Charity itself, where there was excellent supervision. The second year, we were turned loose to the satellite hospitals, where we were in complete charge of the pediatric service. If we encountered an especially difficult case, we would send the child to "Big" Charity by ambulance and hope he would make it. I was assigned to Pineville, in northern Louisiana, and it was pretty frightening to be totally in charge with no one looking over my shoulder.

One case has stayed with me ever since. It concerned a one-month-old baby with a very strange rash, the likes of which I had never seen before. The baby became progressively more ill, and the rash continued to worsen. I finally determined the problem was Letterer-Siwi's disease, a malignant (and always fatal) blood and stem cell disease of unknown cause. I sent him to New Orleans in hope that more could be done there. In two days, he was sent back with the instructions that my diagnosis was correct, but there was nothing they could do.

I explained all I could to the family and told them there was no treatment. The baby was too sick to be cared for at home, so he was kept in the hospital.

I also discovered that this was the sixth child in this family, and that two others had died of similar illnesses, including the rash. There had been no previous diagnosis. Letterer-Siwi's disease was not known to be hereditary. Further investigation was in order.

My wife, Ellen, and I drove to visit the family in their home. There were many relatives present. We worked out the family tree, which was unbelievably intertwined with much intermarriage among the clan. The parents were second cousins two different ways. They treated us with great respect; after all I was "the doctor."

It seems that in 1803, at the time of the Louisiana Purchase, there was a strip of land in what is now northern Louisiana that did not belong to any known government. This lawless area was reportedly settled by runaway slaves, American Indians, and pirates escaping the law. These people began to intermarry and came to be called "Redbones." They were shunned by the surrounding communities, both black and white. This was in the days of school segregation, and they had their own school system. By the 1950s, the community was stabilized at around five thousand people.

The most amazing thing to me was the way the extended family rallied around the baby and his parents. They knew things were hopeless and there was nothing anyone could do. Yet somebody sat by the bedside twenty-four hours a day. There was nowhere for them to sleep, but someone was always awake in the chair over the next two weeks until the baby died. The whole episode was heartbreaking, but I learned what being a family really meant—a lesson that stayed with me the rest of my career.

I never saw a case of Letterer-Siwi's disease again. Charity Hospital was destroyed by Hurricane Katrina.

My Life-Changing Work

Fran Bolos

My husband and I had a pharmacy in Manchester, New Hampshire, that also had medical supplies to keep up with the changing times. In the late 1970s, for the store's best interest, I decided to go to fitting school and learn how to fit people with breast forms and bras as well as orthopedic appliances. I became certified because it was the only way to gain a true knowledge of this aspect of the business. I also believe that you cannot hire people in an aspect of a business without first gaining the firsthand knowledge of the work yourself. My husband was the pharmacist and naturally knew that aspect of the business. I took on the fitting services and so changed the course of our pharmacy forever.

Although the orthopedic appliances were one aspect of the business, I would like to describe my experience working with mastectomy patients. When I initially became trained in that field, I remember telling my husband that I would try it, but I did not know that I would be able to do it so well. All I could think of when I saw a woman in need of my help—and saw the expression on her face—and when she put her arms around me when she was leaving—I cannot explain the feeling of making a difference in a person's life.

When I would meet someone for breast form fitting, I would never wear clothes traditionally associated with medicine, such as white jackets or even a nametag. I knew that my clients had had enough of feeling like patients. I also would make a point of not treating my clients as patients. I have always concentrated on the fashion aspect—to make my clients feel like they were before the mastectomy. Through this work, I have made many longtime friendships.

When we eventually sold the pharmacy in 1997, I decided to open an office and try being on my own. That was thirteen years ago, and my mastectomy fitting business became a semi-retirement business for me. Because of the friendships I have made and the differences I have made to my clients, it is very difficult to give up.

The women I have met are brave women with tremendous courage that had been through a lot before they met me and told me how much I had done for them, when I believe that knowing them has done so much for me.

(Top L to R) Al Harte, Patricia Bray, John Driscoll
Edith Bargar, Paul Leonard
(Seated) Loraley Griffin, Fran Bolos, Edith Yoffa

A Milton Schoolgirl's Journey

Loraley Hogan Griffin

It was September of 1946 when I first walked into the Collicot Elementary School. We had moved to Milton that summer. My dad had managed the First National Store in East Milton and lost his job when it got torn down for the new Southeast Expressway coming right through the square. He decided to buy McKinnon's grocery market on Pleasant Street with a two-story apartment over it. The fact that there would be two schools and Cunningham Park within walking distance for her six children (and a seventh to come) was enough to convince my mother to leave her Colonial in West Quincy and move to the renamed "Hogan's Market." The Collicot secretary registered three Hogans that day: me for third grade, a sister for fourth, and a brother for sixth. My journey with the Milton Schools had begun.

Elementary schools were more carefree in those days. We weren't constantly being tested like the students are today. Right up to sixth grade we would get either S for Satisfactory or U for Unsatisfactory for all our subjects. Penmanship was important enough to have a penmanship teacher come regularly to our classes to teach us the proper slant and size (the Reinhardt System) to our writing. A favorite sixth grade teacher, Miss Tucker, even had us recite a passage from the New Testament each morning and comment on its meaning. This definitely helped me stay on the straight and narrow my whole life, because eleven is a very impressionable age, and I definitely learned right from wrong that year. Students brought bag lunches and ate at their desks. I had to walk to school, home for lunch, and back because I lived less than half a mile away.

I continued on to Mary A. Cunningham Junior High, which was right next door to Collicot. One of the highlights was I could now stay for lunch and eat in the school cafeteria on the third floor with my classmates. At the end of the eighth grade I was expected to choose either a business or a college course for the next four years. The times and large family dictated my choice, which was business. Most female students expected to leave high school and work, so, they would need to learn bookkeeping and shorthand. On the fun side, I practiced all one summer to make the cheerleading team and was picked as the leader of the team, Cunningham, in the ninth grade.

Milton High School was three years, tenth through twelfth in the 1950s. The business courses suited me fine; I worked very hard and excelled. I wore the letter "L" on my MILTON cheerleading sweater and did a lot of yelling while cheering for the basketball and football teams. In my senior year, I was voted the secretary of the Class of 1956. With that came the responsibility of having a class reunion every five years. The best part of reunions, besides seeing friends and reminiscing about all the great school times we had, is to hear all the good that came out of this one class of two hundred students. The different professions, children, grandchildren, and deeds are, as they say, something to write home about, which we asked everyone to do for our fiftieth reunion in 2006.

Now, a step back in time; it was September of 1964 when I walked back into the Collicot Elementary School. This time the secretary registered my daughter for kindergarten and my son for first grade. My daughter was very timid, and the second week of school, the kindergarten teacher told me the fire alarm rang for a fire drill, and she was the only child who cried. The teacher was lining everyone up and trying to explain to them that it was just a practice, but she just didn't buy that. I did remember to explain fire drills when I registered my next two children. My two sons and two daughters all graduated from Milton High School and went on to college. The timid daughter became a preschool and kindergarten teacher! My other daughter taught English but is now a CPA.

I had been a stay-at-home mother for many years, but there came a time, with four colleges ahead, when I had to decide to get back to work. A neighbor of mine really enjoyed her secretarial job at the school department and encouraged me to take a civil service exam so that I could apply there. I hadn't used my shorthand skills for years. I knew my shorthand teacher, Miss Elzbut, was still teaching at Milton High School, so I stopped in to see her to ask if she could lend me the Gregg shorthand book I had used in high school years before. I explained I had to pass a shorthand test at eighty words per minute and needed to practice from the book I learned from because the new books had changed. In that same kind and gentle voice that she had dictated shorthand to me for three years in high school, she replied, "I will have to search in the attic and find it for you." She not only found and sent me that book, she also included some records with dictated shorthand at seventy, eighty, and ninety words per minute with a note advising me to get my speed up to ninety words a minute before I took the test to pass eighty words per minute. What wonderful advice from a very special teacher, and it worked for me.

My memories of being a secretary in three of the Milton schools over a span of twenty-five years are good ones. I used those business skills, and my parenting skills, attending to the needs of the principal, teachers, children, and parents. I enjoyed being back where I had spent such happy years in my own childhood. I tried to always be pleasant and to give back what I had received.

It was August of 1995 when I, again, walked back into the Collicot School. The secretarial position I had held at Milton High School had been eliminated due to budget cuts. The secretary at Collicot was retiring, and I was asked to transfer there. Now, it was me behind the office counter registering all the new Collicot students and incoming kindergarteners. God had brought me full circle. The Collicot School was torn down in 2003, two years after I retired. My oldest son's electrical company installed the solar panels on the new Collicot School and, in April 2010, on the Cunningham School.

My six siblings and I all graduated from Milton High, and two of them became teachers. Nine of our twenty-two children became teachers, and four of them married teachers. Two now teach in Milton. The Hogan mother who is responsible for all these teachers is ninety-two and still lives in Milton, near the Collicot School. Two of her thirty-five great-grandchildren are also teachers and, as the others graduate, we see more teachers in our future. Three of my nine grandchildren are now attending Milton schools.

A Genuine Dogface Soldier

J. Joseph MacIsaac

October 1944: The 103rd Infantry Division of the U.S. Army landed in a cold, damp Marseilles. The division moved up the Rhone Valley on constant alert for enemy resistance. The German army was retreating through a heavily forested area using the foliage as a cover against American air strikes and artillery.

On guard duty one night about 2:00 AM, I positioned myself with my back against a tree, crouching with an M1 rifle between my legs. It was pitch black. While waiting for my relief to arrive and fighting the urge to doze, I was suddenly surprised by something brushing by me a few times. In the darkness, I tried to figure out what it was. Then a whimper from the gloom gave me to understand that it was a dog. I coaxed him into coming closer. He seemed to be delighted with my presence.

He followed me back to our encampment where I placed my poncho over him. In the morning, he shared our rations and attached himself to our squad. He assumed the habit of going on patrol or following whatever the squad was doing at the moment. Whenever we took German prisoners, he would direct a throaty growl at them. He seemed to understand the obligations of being a part of an army, and quickly became the squad pet.

This situation lasted approximately one month until one day while we were being transported via truck, he suddenly stood up straight, raised his head, sprang off the truck, and ran away.

The army convoy stops for no one. We assumed he had reached territory that was familiar to him and ran home. He certainly gave us all some memories of home and was a great companion on long, lonely guard duty nights.

Beloved Dies, House Sold, Fuller Life

Nancy Greene Souther

Is it possible that just six words can describe so effectively the last six years of my life? It would appear so. I am happy to say that my main emotion now is one of deep gratitude. I am grateful to have been able to take care of my husband during his five years of declining health. And I am relieved to have been able to sell my house. Lastly, I am pleased to have made my new home in Fuller Village in Milton, Massachusetts.

After my husband, Louis Cushing Souther, died on Thanksgiving Day of 2003, our home in Canton became an empty shell. During our forty-year span there, it had been a comfortable, happy place. After his death, however, I no longer wanted to remain there. From a practical standpoint, it was too large and required more care than I could provide.

Once all of the legal details were taken care of, I set about getting the house ready for sale. That also meant the downsizing of furnishings and possessions. My first responsibility was to sell Lou's car. I checked on prices of comparable vehicles, wrote an ad, and placed it in one of the local papers. It sold quickly, and that early success gave me the confidence to press on.

Even though I should have been giving some thought to where I would live when the house was sold, I must confess I had not done so; all of my energies had been directed solely toward the sale of the house. I focused on my to-do list all of my waking hours. I was consumed by the job and thought of nothing else. When my sister-in-law, Darcy, remarked, "Nancy, its great that you are making progress around #429, but where are you going once the house has been sold?" I needed to hear that when I did, as I realized I had been avoiding the question out of fear of the unknown. Change is difficult, but I had to face it: I would have to incorporate yet another challenge into my life before completing the task at hand.

Fortunately, I ran into my friend, Mary Moran, at a Stonehill College gathering in 2004. She told me that in June of 2005, she and Jim would be moving to a place called Fuller Village in Milton. It sounded attractive, and the idea of community life was appealing. I looked into it and had the good fortune to meet Ruth Coughlin, a Fuller Village representative. Ruth guided me through the process of acquiring a unit in a caring and professional way. I can now say it is one of the best decisions I have ever made. I moved to Milton on Friday, August 12, 2005, and closed on my Canton home a few days later.

As well as a feeling of security in my new surroundings, a truly rewarding facet of my new life has been pleasure. I had been involved in Lou's care for more than five years. Then, after his death, getting the house ready for sale took almost two years of intense work. During that period, I had not been socializing. It was a new friend, Jane Dooley, who, when she found out we were both going to be living in the same building at Fuller Village, said, "Oh, Nancy, we are going to have so much fun!" I can remember the moment clearly as I digested her delightful message. Fun was a concept that had been missing from my life for more than half a decade, and how refreshing it was to hear the promise of it. Jane and John Dooley have more than fulfilled that commitment in our four years here.

Another memorable occasion occurred when, shortly after we all moved into Building F, Jack and Nancy Kearns hosted a Sunday afternoon "get acquainted" party in their large, welcoming unit. They gave each of us an opportunity to introduce ourselves to one another and to describe our former lives and missing loved ones. Nancy and Jack orchestrated things deftly with grace, humor, and gentle encouragement. From that day on, we became caring friends and neighbors. I couldn't be happier in the new home I have chosen. In every sense of the word, it has indeed given me a fuller life, and I remain deeply grateful.

It's All About Faith

Jack Kearns

Life is a challenge, as we all know. We somehow live through all the highs and lows, with a little bit of luck added to the mix in order to survive. But many of us like to believe the most important ingredient in the recipe is faith!

In my young years, growing up in St. Ann's Parish in Dorchester, I enjoyed a lot of pick-up sports. Baseball was easily my favorite. I played for Christopher Columbus High School in the North End. I was left-handed and was told that I could throw the ball hard. One day, after I had pitched a no-hitter, a scout from the Brooklyn Dodgers approached me and offered me the opportunity to play in their farm league in Canada; my life took off!

It was a very exciting time for me at age seventeen to then play a couple of years in the minors. The opportunity, however, did come to an end. I came back to earth and soon played in the Boston Park League for ten years while in college and afterward. I was drafted to serve in the army for two years. As luck and talent would have it, I played in Korea and Japan. Our faith was tested when our games were interrupted by incoming fire from North Korea. I was proud to later be inducted into the Boston Park League Hall of Fame. To this day, I meet my pals at the annual banquet where we relive and embellish on our memorable moments. I am now on the Selection Committee and help choose the new players to keep this great tradition alive.

During this period of time, I met my first love. Pat and I were married in 1961 and soon were blessed with five children: three boys and two girls. After awhile, we sold our two-family house in Dorchester and bought a single home in East Milton. It was across from Andrews Park where the kids spent most of their free time playing a great variety of sports.

Then, in 1981, I received the phone call that filled me with fear. Pat had been diagnosed with cancer, and my life took a terrible turn. Pat passed away on Thanksgiving Day three years later. My faith was tested, but the kids, then high school age, and I survived.

As I mentioned earlier, you have to have faith! Twenty-five years ago, my life's journey took a very good turn. I met Nancy, whose husband, Charlie, had died around the same time as Pat. Imagine how nervous we were on our first date! We were married on July 2, 1989, and had our reception on the *Spirit of Boston*, sailing on Boston Harbor. With Nancy's four sons joining my five teen and twenty-somethings, the new *Brady Bunch* was formed. Soon, with nine kids and nine cars, we moved into a bigger home. You've got to have faith!

During the next fifteen years, the kids gradually left the nest, were married, and settled nearby. We were then the proud grandparents of twenty and didn't want to host any more huge holiday parties. It was time for us to move on, and we are now very happily living in Fuller Village. Our faith is still very strong. We are enriched by an amazing group of neighbors and wonderful new friends.

You've got to have faith!

Life Is Not Linear

Myrtle R. Flight

"Oh, no, not again; they were here just last week!" my mother cried as Leona and Gertrude pulled up in front of the house and unpacked their bagpipes. Of course, it was suppertime. Dad would invite them to stay and get his fiddle. The music would start. My sister and I would run into the bedroom, cover our heads with blankets and hide until supper; "finnan haddie" (smoked haddock) was on the table. Other times my father's friends would come over to play the spoons, harmonica, jazz flute, piano, zither, ukulele, etc. One warm summer night, all the cats in the neighborhood gathered around the porch to yowl in a supporting chorus. This was my introduction to music.

Leona, the sister of my father's mother, lived in Nova Scotia. Gertrude was her daughter. When I married Curtis Flight from Milton, I did not know that his mother's family came from Nova Scotia and lived fifteen miles from the "new world" origins of my father's clan. Curt's father came from Saint John's, Newfoundland, and finnan haddie was the dish eaten at most family gatherings. "Ugh!"

When I was a child, my dad would often take me for tea at his mother's on Thursday afternoon. She and her husband, Gaius, lived on Rosebury Road in the Rugby section of Hyde Park. Grandma Alice was known for her ability to tell fortunes from tea leaves. Once a week, her followers would line up outside the house, climb the stairs to the second floor, and find out what their future held. The house was dark inside, and there was the odor of incense. Chipped "old English" china cups with tea leaves resting on the bottom were set on a round table with a muted light resting inside a lamp. Once a month, Alice read the fortune of the governor of Massachusetts, James Michael Curley, when he made the rounds of Rugby to see his constituents.

We moved into Milton when I was six or seven. There were too many bodies to fit into the Cummings Highway apartment, and number three child was on the way. My mother's mother, Lotta Cushman, rented an apartment on River Street in Mattapan, and we would walk to visit her two or three times a week. "Lot," as she was known, was of English/Scottish background. Her father published books, and her mother was a seamstress. Lot was divorced and made extra money decorating hats. My sister, Claire, and I would help with the hats. The hats were large straw frames decorated with multicolored flowers and ribbons. My sister and I would sit at the dining room table and sew petals on the frames, and when we completed the quota, Lot would put them in net sacks and take them to the market in New York.

While we were working, the egg man would come, the iceman, Cushman's bakery truck, and the ragman. We could hear the trolleys pass by on the street every so many minutes.

Lot loved Filene's Basement and purchased her clothes there. On one occasion, she found a table full of black crepe dresses with white lines sketched as a pattern for only one dollar. She bought two: final sale. At home, after closer examination of the purchase, Lot determined the design included nude women. Again, my sister and I were brought to the dining room table with directions to cover the white lines with black permanent ink to make the dresses "decent."

During this time period, my mother designed and sewed dresses for women with "difficult-to-fit" physiques. My father, Clarence, was a butcher. During the hunting season, he would cut up deer and wrap them up in paper for hunters' freezers.

When I was a child, I taught school in the garage from the age of six years on. During the summer, every morning the neighborhood kids would come to our backyard and play school—the beginning of my professional career. Our family was among the first to get a television set. In the late afternoon, the "class" would come in to our living room, with the overflow looking in the window, and watch *Howdy Doody* and *Mr. Roberts*.

From Milton High School, I went to Colby Junior College (CJC) in New London, New Hampshire. My dad gave me the choice of three careers: teacher, secretary or nurse. I was allowed to go to CJC because, at that time, it was affiliated with the Baptists. There I had to be in my room by nine o'clock on weeknights and could not go anywhere without written permission from my dad on weekends. Consequently, I came home to Boston every weekend, and met my husband in Milton, Massachusetts.

After two years at Colby Junior, I returned to Milton and became a secretary for Alexander Nadas, chief of pediatric cardiology at Children's Hospital in Boston. I later married, had two children (Curtis and Linda), and went back to school at Northeastern University nights, then law school. I went to New England School of Law (NESL) beginning at the age of forty-two. My goal: Try a case before fifty.

My interest in law began as a young child during a sailing excursion in Marblehead with a lawyer friend of my father. Law entered my life again during my first teaching job at Aquinas Junior College in Milton. I was teaching a course for a new program, Medical Assisting, with Sister Winifred Kelly. We were teaching without texts, clinical or legal. Sister Winifred suggested that I write the legal textbook while she would write the clinical. Together, we visited numerous physicians offices in Milton and surrounding towns, accepted their castoff medical magazines, and began to cut and paste. Soon the pile of paper became too high, and the subject too confusing; I moved to another position in health services at Blue Hill Regional Vocational Technical School. The legal text, however, remained piled on the corner of my desk.

True to fashion, I had millions of ideas for Blue Hills' students. The course grew, my job grew, and I was approached to take the job of assistant director of vocational subjects. I applied and was assured I would get the job. The day the appointment was made, however, the position was given to a man whose qualifications did not come close to mine. But he was a man!

After I was informed, I put on my coat and walked out. When I got home, my husband Curt appealed to reason, and the next day I returned to Blue Hills. I was secretary to the local teachers union at that time, under contract, and I filed a request to submit the matter to arbitration. The union turned me down.

The next step was to appeal to the state organization, the Massachusetts Teachers Association (MTA). Their response: "This is a nuisance case." At this point, according to our contract, I had the right to hire my own attorney. At the time, the Massachusetts Federation of Teachers was trying to become the representative for the state's regional vocational schools; in light of that, I hired the Massachusetts Federation of Teachers attorney, Allen McDonald.

Attorney McDonald won every step of the way: The District School Committee, the arbitration hearings, the Norfolk County Superior Court, the Massachusetts Appellate Court, and the Superior Judicial Court of Massachusetts. At this point, the District School Committee had exhausted their case before the Massachusetts courts and turned to fabricate constitutional issues for the United States Supreme Court (USSC).

The case dragged on for five years. During this time, our family ate a lot of spaghetti, and I learned about the way lawyers operate. I knew that at any time I could lose the case, and Sister Winifred's dream book still lay untouched on the corner of my desk.

Four plus years into the matter, the (USSC) returned the case to the DSC, allowing the Massachusetts decision in my favor to stand. The DSC could not take defeat and decided to file another appeal with the USSC. The individuals on the DSC were not paying for their own legal fees. Attorney McDonald filed a Massachusetts case against each individual DSC member; that meant they would have to hire lawyers individually and pay from their own pockets. They settled in five days, and I received the job, the back pay, and a lot of publicity and self-satisfaction.

I remained in the job until my children graduated from college. I passed the bar and practiced almost twenty-five years. I have taught approximately thirty-five years in some capacity in the Blue Hill Regional Massasoit Community College complex, and the fifth edition of *Law, Liability and Ethics,* Sister Winifred's dream, came onto the market the first of July 2010.

Sleep Apnea

Gerard J. "Jerry" Joyce

At the age of seventy-two, I had prostate cancer cured by radiation at Massachusetts General Hospital. Then I started having what I thought were kidney problems, for many years growing worse each year. I was getting up ten or more times at night to go to the bathroom. I was falling asleep during the day, my memory was failing me, and my children were driving me crazy wanting me to stop driving. Finally, I had a little accident that was my fault. My thinking, reasoning, and memory got so bad that I was beginning to lose confidence in myself.

Then my doctor sent me to a specialist for an examination. This doctor gave me a detailed thorough exam. At the end, he said I definitely had Alzheimer's. It was mild but would get progressively worse. He said there was no doubt about it, and he started me on a pill that might slow it down. My own doctor gave me a lot of samples but, eventually, I could not tolerate the pill.

Meanwhile, I called the Veterans Administration for a prescription. The V.A. said they would not give me the prescription unless I saw a V.A. doctor. When I saw that doctor, he gave me the exact same exam as the other doctor, down to a "T." However, at the end he said I had dementia, but it was not Alzheimer's. Boy, was I happy! The V.A. doctor said he didn't know what the dementia was but would hopefully find out.

Eventually, the doctor had me go to the V.A. in Brockton where I would sleep overnight for testing. They concluded I had sleep apnea. The heart has to get oxygen constantly. Sleep apnea is caused by the oxygen to the heart being interrupted, causing the person to wake up. Some people who snore have this problem. I was one of them.

I now wear a facemask with a machine that warms distilled water, causing a steady flow of air to my heart through my mouth. As soon as I started wearing this mask, my memory and reasoning abruptly returned. I was a new man! Medically speaking, it was the best thing that ever happened to me in my life except for my bypass surgery twenty-five years ago.

Even Good Guys Get into Trouble

John J. "Jack" McCarthy

Captain Harold Ruble, although just a lieutenant, was the skipper—the man in command and a veteran navy man, having been a chief quartermaster before the war. With the great need for experienced skippers, the navy commissioned a lot of these regular navy enlisted men as ensigns and lieutenants junior grade to command the many ships that were being built to fight the war. These officers were called "mustangs." I don't know the significance of that name, but that's what they were called.

Of course, being an ex-enlisted man, Captain Ruble knew every trick in the book and was not about to let anything be pulled on him. He therefore ran a very tight ship. Seldom did a week go by that he did not hold a Captain's Mast or Summary Court-Martial. A reading of the official ship's log shows that sixty of the less than one hundred enlisted men and two officers were brought before the Captain's Mast for punishment, and many of these sixty appeared three or four times. Six were given a Summary Court-Martial and twelve of the enlisted men went AWOL.

I was not exempt from this ritual, which was usually held when we were running empty after dropping off troops and equipment at some beach and were heading back to pick up more troops and supplies for the next invasion. It didn't matter to the captain if we were in enemy waters or not; as long as we were not carrying troops, he would hold his Captain's Mast. Case in point, the log from February 21, 1945, shows DD499, the USS *Renshaw,* which was protecting our convoy, was struck by a Japanese torpedo on her port side while Captain Ruble held court. He didn't let anything interfere with his tight-fisted control of the ship.

Among the offenses were sleeping on watch, disobedience of an order, swearing, fighting, drunkenness, inattention to duty, having someone else's clothing in your locker, etc. I was able to go from the date of my enlistment, August 6, 1943, until February 6, 1945, a total of eighteen months, without getting into trouble, but on February 7, 1945, the ship's log recorded that I was brought up on charges. Specifically, it states that I was inattentive to duty and disobeyed an order. For that, I was given ten hours of extra duty and demoted to seaman second class. What did I do to deserve this? I don't recall; I must have been told to do something that I thought was stupid and wrong.

My second offense came one week later. This one was unique; it was the only time this offense showed up in the logs of either the LST 910 or LST 912. It was listed as "Violation of Censorship Regulations." Now here we are in the middle of the Pacific, thousands of miles from the nearest telephone and with the radio controlled and monitored twenty-four hours a day seven day a week. In addition, all outgoing mail had to be censored by an officer before being sent stateside. What in the world did I do to deserve this charge? I'll tell you what happened.

As a quartermaster, my position on board ship was in the wheelhouse, both while on watch (every day four hours on and eight hours off) and at general quarters (whenever the ship was under attack or the threat of an attack). That is where the ship's command and control is. The wheelhouse is just above the officers' quarters, and there is a ladder leading directly from their quarters to the chart room. The chart room is directly aft of the wheelhouse and forward of the radio room.

Now, I was on the midnight to 4:00 AM watch in the chart room, which had low lighting because the ship was always running in darkness; no lights were to show or be visible on deck or topside. So there I was, writing away at the chart table when the skipper came quietly up the ladder around 2:00 AM. I immediately tried to hide what I was doing. Had I continued as if I was doing nothing wrong, I'm sure nothing would have happened. But since he saw me trying to hide what I was writing, he then wanted to see what it was. Upon recognizing that it was my personal journal, he immediately put me on report.

I had been keeping a journal for some time, my own personal log of where we had been, including my thoughts and reactions to the Kamikaze plane attacks, the sub attacks, and the various invasions we had been on. At that time during the war, this was a major no-no. We were not allowed to keep a journal or to take pictures or possess anything that would indicate where we had been or what we had done. The purpose of that prohibition was to deny the enemy any intelligence in case we were captured. It seems ridiculous now in the age of GPS, satellites, digital cameras, computers, and the Internet, but that was the way it was sixty-five years ago.

I'm always amazed at my shipmates who came home with pictures. Every picture that I have of my time in the service is a copy, thanks to someone else's ability to avoid being brought up on charges of "Violation of Censorship Regulations".

(Top L to R) Hy Rossen, Sharon and Bob La Bree
Ellen and Tom White
(Seated) Gwen Senger, Anna Gerut, Anne Gebhardt

The Beach

Janet Arthur

Our family of seven used to pile into our station wagon and go to our special beach, Cockle Cove in South Chatham, Cape Cod, Massachusetts. A saltwater marsh sat calmly on the left side of the winding road to the beach. A blue heron sometimes stood in the marsh water. We could see the ocean at the end of the road. On the horizon was a row of fish weir. The sky was as clear as it was blue with the ocean that met it an even deeper shade of azure.

Eel River flowed between the beach and the ocean, and it wandered into the marsh as well. There was a wooden footbridge over the river that was used to get to the sandy ocean beach. The water in the river was always warm and shallow. It was the perfect place in which to float small boats or to just paddle around looking for fiddler crabs and small blue crabs. The boys used crab nets on long wooden handles to capture the blue crabs. One day, Jimmy caught a blue crab with an intact one-dollar bill in its claw. You can imagine how excited he was!

We carried a colorful striped beach umbrella, a few straw mats, and a simple lunch (it might just be peanut butter sandwiches and a drink) as we crossed over the bridge to the outer sandy beach. Eating lunch on the beach was sometimes a challenge to keep sand from blowing into the sandwiches.

After lunch there was time to play in the ocean, jump the waves, and build sandcastles. The children could hunt for seashells and horseshoe crabs or just run around chasing each other, trying all the while not to kick sand on other beachgoers. The adults would relax on the straw mats under the beach umbrella.

Our family enjoyed many trips to Cockle Cove Beach through the years because we really came to see Gramma and Grampa Fuller who eventually retired to their home there.

Gramma would come to the beach with our family and carried her own beach chair. I recently had a vision of her in which she was wearing a skirt-style bathing suit with a dark print and lighter floral design. She had on a pointed straw hat with fringe around the wide brim (perhaps she had purchased it on a trip to Puerto Rico, but I'm not sure). Her sunglasses were large and round with plastic rims and bows. In my vision she is sitting in her green webbed sand chair and her legs are covered with a beach towel.

While we were enjoying the beach scene, Grampa was back at the house doing his Saturday chores. Then he would listen to the Red Sox game. When we came back to the house, we would usually find him sitting in his Boston rocker; I still have his chair. I always wished Grampa (my dad) would come to the beach with all of us, but we made time to visit with him before we started the trip back to our home in Canton, Massachusetts.

Eyewitness to a Successful Stroke Recovery

Jane Dooley

On February 28, 2009, I was awakened at 2:30 AM by my husband, John, who was in bed beside me. He was mumbling and not making any sense. I knew right away that something was wrong. He was trying to get up to go to the bathroom but was having trouble walking. When he came back, he also knew something was not right. I asked him to raise his arms together, which he could not do. Then I asked him to stick out his tongue; he did not do it correctly. I asked him his name and what was the date. I don't know what made me do all this, but I had a sense of calmness about me. I knew he was having a stroke, so I got two baby aspirin from the medicine cabinet and told him to sit down on the bed. He took the aspirin. I told him to stay calm and that I was going to call 911. He said, "No, I don't need 911." but I told him to just relax and I would take care of everything. He did and I called.

The resort security arrived in five minutes. We have a new hospital almost across the street from where we live in the winter in Destin, Florida. The EMTs arrived in fifteen minutes along with a fire engine, the police, and an ambulance. I was so glad to see them, and they took over. After talking to him, they told me to go to the hospital in my car, and they would follow right behind.

When I got to the hospital, they started giving John tests. He did not have a doctor in Destin, as he was never sick. That was a big mistake on my part. That is fixed now, and we both see doctors regularly that we like. The hospital called a stroke doctor. He started him immediately on the correct medicine and suggested more tests. John did not get that shot that many people get within a two-hour period as they did not know how long before he had the stroke as he was sleeping.

During this time, John was very quiet. He could talk but was not making much sense. In the hospital, he was in a bed that was very uncomfortable for him, and he couldn't wait to go home. On the third day, they let him sit up. They finally released him after three days. Several nurses visited him three times a week, as well as a physical therapist, an occupational therapist, and a speech therapist. All were wonderful and encouraged him to exercise every day, and they gave him lots of exercises to do to get better.

John was amazing. He started following right away all the directions they gave him. His priority was clear and focused: to get better. He restructured his day to make sure he got all his exercises done. He got up at 7:00 AM, had his coffee, and then went straight to the gym. He worked out for one and a half hours, riding the bike and doing weights, then came back and had his breakfast. He made sure to rest every day in the afternoon. The doctors told him that was part of the therapy. But then he went right back to it and started on his stretching, hitting golf balls, writing, or speaking out loud looking in a mirror. Within three weeks, he got rid of the walker and then the cane, but he had a lot of trouble speaking, writing, and swallowing his food and drink.

We had to add a thickener to his liquids and also to some of his food, so they would go down the right tube. He hated that! He read tongue twisters out loud as part of his speech therapy. He made funny faces with his mouth and had to stretch his jaw in every direction to make his mouth work correctly again. He started to lose weight, which wasn't a bad thing. He had been in good shape before the stroke, as he exercised and stretched almost every day. He had been playing golf about five days a week and was walking when he played. He did not take any medicine and was very proud of that. The doctors said his good physical shape before the stroke helped lessen the effects of the stroke and aided his recovery time.

So why did this happen to a man who seemed to be in such great shape? John's friends and family were shocked that this had happened. He did not seem like a likely stroke candidate. We might never know the reason, but we knew that there was a lot to do to get better, so we focused on that. Every day he did what he was told to do. He started to improve. After a month, he could see a difference. After three months, he was better, and after six months, then nine months, then a year. He had to buy new clothes, which he did not like to do; his old clothes were perfectly good. He read everything on strokes that he could get his hands on. He reread all the instructions of the doctors. The doctors continued to see improvement each time John went to see them.

John began walking each morning. When he first started, he wasn't sure he could make it back home, but he stuck with it. Gradually, he got stronger and walked further. The more he walked, the more endurance he developed. I watched all this and was so impressed. He didn't tell me that he was so nervous about walking until about three weeks after he started.

He went to the gym every day. At first a friend went with John and stayed with him while he did his exercise routine. Everyone at the gym knew he had had a stroke, and they watched him. They would watch him and then whisper to me that he was doing better. He never missed a day. He had always been an athlete and a long time coach, so he knew the value of exercise, and he stuck with it. The amazing thing to me as I watched him get better was his attitude. He kept his good sense of humor, which made my life easier too.

John's brothers and sister would call him several times a day, and, of course, his children were so concerned and were writing to him and encouraging him all the time. He was giving it right back to them, telling them he was doing great and feeling so much better. His attitude helped them get through this and was so tremendous for me. One of his favorite expressions before and still is, "Make each day a quality day."

John wanted to return to golf, so he went to the golf club every day and practiced. His buddies at the club encouraged him. He would hit, but his right hand and side didn't cooperate. He stuck with it, but it was very hard. Some of them told me they never thought he would play again. They watched him and gave him encouragement.

All of our friends and many others asked for details on what had happened and what I did to react that very first night. They also wanted to know what happened next, how he responded to therapy, and what exercises he did. I knew they were thinking that it could have been them. I tried to give people who asked key details to help them and to spread the word on what worked for us to help lessen the effect of the stroke.

We returned home to Milton in the spring, and John continued his workout routine. If he couldn't make the gym, then he worked out in another way. The pool was one of his favorite activities. He tried to swim every day. He said that everything he did each day was part of his therapy. He learned how to do the laundry. He was always a good cook, so he continued cooking.

John is a wonderful father, and there is nothing he would not do for his children and grandchildren. So he would run errands for them, go watch swim meets, baseball, softball, and gymnastic events. He is now back to playing eighteen holes of golf, although he says he will never return to his "greatness."

It has now been one year and five months. I always knew he was a good man, but the strength and determination he has shown during this ordeal have been amazing. I am very proud of John and consider myself very lucky to have found such a wonderful guy.

"Hi, Miss Paula"

Paula Silbert

The tapestry of my life has been a journey, a journey of truly wonderful events and many not so. But, throughout the journey, the highlight has always been my family. After all of my children married and had children of their own, this extended part of my life became even more meaningful and precious.

But now I was faced with the dilemma of time on my hands. What to do with that newly acquired time that would be meaningful and rewarding? In thinking about it, I realized how much I had always enjoyed working with people. I had studied education in college and thoroughly enjoyed working with children in a library setting.

I began using the computer for research, searching areas of interest to me. And I came across a nonprofit organization called Generations, Inc. What this group did was to send volunteers over age fifty-five into the Boston Public Schools to assist the faculties. Volunteers helped out as reading coaches to enhance classroom literacy. I well remember to this day being greeted with, "Hi, Miss Paula" from the teachers and wonderful students I worked with. The Generations program left a great impact on both the volunteers and the children.

Life has come full circle—I have raised my children, served as teacher, and live in a community here at Fuller Village that is comfortable and friendly. So, when you see me, please say, "Hi, Miss Paula." It evokes lovely memories for me.

Memorial

J. Alexander Harte

I started flagging Milton cemetery for the American Legion in 1956 in preparation for Memorial Day. After a few years, I took over the complete job. I received many calls on missed Veteran's flags due to missing bronze makers or other identification.

My son was looking for an Eagle Scout project, so I came up with the idea to have him go through the cemetery files and mark the locations on the old maps of all the veteran's lots. This enabled us to identify all the grave lots that needed to be flagged.

Recently, a government survey made new maps of all the new sections that had been added since I started. I transferred all the information I had to the new maps. These maps are now kept up to date. There are approximately 2,500 veteran's lots, and they are rapidly increasing.

Over the years, I have had some help from my granddaughters, Katie and Kim. Many members of the legion also helped at various times to complete the flagging prior to Memorial Day.

At some point in time, I noticed something was wrong. The veterans' lot had a flat stone marker labeled SOLDIERS LOT. I talked this over with the cemetery superintendent, and we agreed this was not an appropriate memorial, as all service branches were located there. He talked it over with the cemetery directors, and they agreed. We then had a suitable stone procured. In the meantime, a new cemetery superintendent, Mrs. Sills, was appointed; she helped me expedite the project. I then had a meeting with the legion to make the necessary funds available so that the project could continue.

A company was contacted to help us design and make the plaque that was to be mounted on the stone. When it arrived, we had it mounted on the stone with the legion emblem on the left side below the plaque. I was also able to replace the old deteriorated wooden flagpole with a new maintenance-free, plastic flagpole behind the stone.

The plaque reads as follows:

THIS MEMORIAL IS DEDICATED TO THE MEMORY
OF THOSE MEN AND WOMEN FROM THE TOWN
OF MILTON WHO SERVED THEIR COUNTRY IN
THE ARMED SERVICES. THEY LIE HERE IN MUTE
TESTIMONY TO THE MANNER IN WHICH THEY
LIVED, WORKED, AND FOUGHT TO ACHIEVE THE
VICTORIES IN ORDER THAT AMERICA MAY LIVE FREE.

I had the pleasure of dedicating and presenting the American Legion's donation to the Town of Milton on Memorial Day 1989.

A Family Remembered

Anna Gerut

I was born in Lodz, Poland. I come from a middle class family of eight. My parents were very well educated. My father was a scholar with two rabbinical diplomas. Our life was based on religion, education, honesty, and generosity. The members of my family are as follows (1942): Father, Rabbi Nechemiah Warszawski, age forty-eight; Mother, Rajzla Warszawski (b. Weinstein) age forty-six.

There were six children and I was the oldest: Chana (myself); Ammanuel, brother, age eighteen; Moshe, brother, age sixteen; Esther-Brucha, sister, age fourteen (survived until last year); Szlamek, brother, age ten; and Naomi, sister, age eight.

My sister Esther-Brucha and I were the only survivors of a family of more than one hundred relatives. Last year, I lost this precious, dearest sister too. What a tragedy this is for me now.

When I was a teenager I studied a poem by a Polish poet, Julius Slowacki, "Ojciec Zadzumionych," a story where a man lost his wife and children from a contagious disease. I cried every time I read how he suffered after every child's death. I could not understand how a person could go through such tragedies. Now I am the one who has gone through this horrible suffering. I lost my family because they were Jewish. Hitler (*Imach szymoy*) had to get rid of the Jews. For us there is no happy ending. On every occasion, happy or sad, I miss my family.

Since I am now the only survivor of the Warszawski family, I would like to mention my grandfather, Henoch Warszawski. He lived with his very large family in a little town near Warsaw called Jeziorna. He was a very well known personality and was the representative from this vicinity. He was well-known for his generosity. On his property, he donated a prayer house and a school for children (*Cheder)*, and whoever had no place to live stayed at his house. He died just before

World War II and was taken for burial to Ger (*Gora Kalwarja)* where the Rabbi from Ger (Rabbi Alter) could attend his funeral. All the stores were closed. The rabbi of Ger visited my grandfather when he was sick in Jeziorna. There were many articles about his generosity after his death. I took all the papers and pictures with me to Auschwitz.

After the war I was told that my uncle Pinchus Warszawski was in the Warsaw Ghetto Uprising. He was sent along with his family to Treblinka. Also sent to Treblinka were my father's sister and her husband Moshe Applebaum (the editor of the Jewish newspaper *Der Moment*) with their three children. Sorry that America did not take in these beautiful people before it was too late. Everything is gone. What a loss!

About myself, I went through a horrible time in the Litzmanstadt ghetto where I lost my family in 1942. My brother Emmanuel wrote in the ghetto, "It is easier to write a book" than to live through one day in the ghetto where so many people die from hunger; for us to live through a day in the ghettos or concentration camps was a miracle.

The next hell was Auschwitz. It is a horrible and unbelievable story—hard to believe or understand for people who were not there. Hitler's (*Imach Shimoy*) motto was to get rid of the Jewish nation. My nightly dreams of horror come constantly, seeing the young members of my family suffering. It is very hard for me to write about and relive this tragic time.

My husband, Leibel Fingerhut (Gerut) from Oswirciany, Lithuania, was in the Shavel ghetto and was then sent to Dachau. He lost his parents: Rachel and Zachariah Fingerhut (a cantor in the Shul) and his brothers and sisters. Now he suffers from an incurable illness due to the sufferings of his life.

Our story is like a drop in the ocean and cannot be told in one day or in one night. I remember my father telling us the story of Jewish slavery from the Haggadah on Pesach. I never could have believed that I would be one of the tragic persons of Jewish history.

We have to thank America for its freedom. We brought up two highly educated children, Rosalie and Zachary Emmanuel. They are an asset to our community, and we hope they will have a happy life.

We hope there will be no more wars. After the wars, no one is a winner. Because of our dearest victims, the six million

Kiddoshim, we got back our country, Israel. We must remember to support her. Our fathers were praying every day with the words "Shema Yisrael," and we must say "Am Yisrael Chai"!!

My Life

Josephine Ferruggio

I have loved my life. Growing up in my family has left me with wonderful memories that always warm my heart. Our neighborhood in South Boston was friendly and supportive; it was always "open house" at our house. The whole family loved visitors, and our yard, which was the only one in the neighborhood, was often full of neighbor children playing on the swings and splashing in our pool. My mom, who worked as a chocolate dipper at Schrafft's, would bring home candies for us and our friends. Mom taught us generosity; she was always there in the kitchen preparing food for us and our ever-present visitors. I still can see her making that homemade ravioli and cacciatore. Even when she got old, there she was cooking while seated in her wheelchair.

Our yard was like a mini farm; my folks grew vegetables, among them tomatoes, zucchini, and peppers. There was a nectarine tree and two peach trees that Mom grew from seeds. My dad tended the fig tree and the concord grape arbor that kept our neighbor well supplied for his winemaking.

But the central attraction at our house was Lucky, our pet tortoise. Dad had brought her up from Florida on one of his trips to buy fruit for his business. He said he found her crossing the street. She had a beautiful brown shell and was about a foot long, eventually growing to about 2 feet. All of us kids adored her; the little ones would ride her or stand on her back, but she never seemed to mind. I can still see my mom feeding Lucky spaghetti with a fork! Sometimes we would put her in the tub for a swim and she could signal by scratching that she wanted out.

One day Lucky disappeared from the yard; we were terrified that an automobile would end her days. All the neighbors were searching for her, but I was the one who found her across the street. At first, she appeared to be a big rock lying in the middle of the sidewalk, but, thank heaven, it was really Lucky. Lucky, lucky, lucky us! Another time Lucky fell from our second-floor porch and cracked her shell. My sister cleaned her up with peroxide and taped her shell, and, would you believe, she healed fine. In later years, Lucky moved with us to Randolph Avenue in Milton where she was eventually laid to rest. We had thought she was about 80 years old, but my sister found out from the vet that she was actually 160!

When I went to work, I had several different kinds of jobs in sales and garment work. I liked it best where I could use my sewing skills, and I was fascinated with the process of creating clothing. I worked with designers and pattern drafters to make men's suits and women's dresses, and the whole process seemed fascinating: designing the garment, drafting the pattern, cutting it from the fabric, fitting the cutout on the form, checking the fit, and reworking the imperfections.

Buyers and supervisors came to check the product, and they almost always found some. When the fit was perfected and the pattern was ready, then came the time for grinding out the copies. It was so gratifying to see the finished product. Yes, it was hard work and often tedious, but I enjoyed it.

I loved it all, and it's been a good life. True, it was hard, and many who have had much more than I have had will complain mightily. But I remember the good times, the challenging jobs I had, the fun, how hard I worked, and how I always tried to do my best.

Boston's Wish-You-Were-Here Guys

Alan Klein

After serving in the navy in World War II, graduating from the University of Rhode Island, and working in the lumber business, I got a middle-management job in a large postcard factory. My title was customer service manager. One of my duties was to supervise the insignificant local distribution and boost sales of postcards in the Boston area as well as to be involved with every kind of problem with postcard distributors around the world!

When competition from Asia seriously hurt manufacturers of just about all products made in the United States, the company I worked for eliminated a layer of middle management. When I found myself suddenly unemployed, I started my own postcard distributorship.

I was not a great photographer, but I knew good photos when I saw them, and I had a photographer friend who was good with his camera and was the photographer for the Boston Police Department. He agreed to take as many pictures as he could in one day for $50.00 if I drove him to the photo sites, paid for the film and processing, and bought him lunch.

With the photos in hand, I ordered a line of postcards from my former employer's largest competitor for delivery around the first of the year. My new stock in trade did not arrive until March, along with a bill for $5,000 that was due in April. This was money I did not have.

I called the manufacturer and told him that since they were six weeks late in delivery, I would take six weeks longer to pay the bill. The new postcards were beautifully printed, and the new photos were far better than those on the market. They were promptly sold, paid for, and reordered.

My son, Jonathan, joined me as our salesman, developed an interest in photography, and became an excellent photographer. Postcards, guidebooks, maps, and souvenirs were quickly added to our line. Back in the 1970s, postcards were an important product. There was no Internet, and long-distance phone calls were expensive. The tourist photos were not nearly so good and inexpensive, and there was no way to get maps on GPS systems.

After working out of my basement in Hyde Park, I bought the former Salvation Army Building on Harvard Avenue in Hyde Park. Jonathan now runs the business together with his wife, Wendy. He has the support of my wife, Sally, and is also occasionally helped by his sister, Janet, and his brother, Andrew. “Jon” still takes the pictures, many of which have won awards of excellence from the International Postcard Distributors. Far more than half of the company’s revenue now comes from souvenirs like coffee mugs, magnets, key-chains, snow globes, and our well-known calendars.

Back in the 1970s and 1980s, we were selling well over a million postcards a year to tourists. These cards not only carried the beautiful images of our city, but were also emblazoned with the written endorsement, “Having a wonderful time, wish you were here.” These millions of cards over many years have enticed hordes of people to come to our area, and the souvenirs certainly reminded folks from around the world of pleasant memories of Boston.

Today Jonathan occasionally asks me to deliver merchandise on the South Shore. I am also asked for advice on business matters. I guess that if one starts an institution, works hard to help it grow and succeed, one never really retires from it. Every once in a while, I wish I were still there!

A Day in Federal Court

Michael W. Ryan

In the Spring of 1964, my wife, Shirley, and I packed our 1960 Nash Rambler station wagon, loaded our four pre-school age children in the tailgate, and proceeded to drive to my first duty station as a newly assigned U.S. Postal Inspector. That duty station, Hazard, Kentucky, was determined by the flip of a coin a few months earlier in the office of the postal inspector in charge. I lost the coin toss to a classmate who chose Middlesboro, Kentucky, the only other option and a far more urbane community.

As lifelong residents of the Chicago area, Shirley and I would find eastern Kentucky to be a great learning experience, culturally and otherwise, and one that would prepare us for the relocations we were to periodically experience throughout my career. To give a sense of it, while the rest of the country was listening to 1964 classics such as The Temptations' "The Way You Do The Things You Do", residents of eastern Kentucky were hooked on Jim Nesbitt's "Lookin' for more in '64", which began, "Say there, buddy, do you have the price of a soft drink on ya?"

Our rented bungalow was situated across the road from the North Fork Kentucky River and a railroad yard that, we would quickly learn, functioned as a staging area for coal cars, frequently operating in the dead of night. As soon as we were settled into our new home and a supply of food had been laid up in the pantry, I took up my duties that mainly consisted of auditing post offices and investigating postal crimes such as mail thefts and post office burglaries. As luck would have it, I discovered my first post office embezzlement on my first day in my new assignment. The postmaster had failed to account for about $850 in money order sales and insisted she had "lost" the money. My review of the cashbook told another story, however, and she was subsequently charged with embezzling post office funds. A few months later, the postmaster was called to appear in federal court in Jackson, Kentucky, to answer the charges.

Located more or less in the heart of the Eastern Kentucky coal fields, the federal court in Jackson was the site of numerous prosecutions for violations of federal laws governing the distilling of whiskey. Those who built and operated illegal distilleries were referred to as moonshiners or bootleggers, and eastern Kentucky was rife with them. Aside from me, the only other federal law enforcement officers stationed in Hazard were two Alcohol, Tobacco and Firearms (ATF) agents who were responsible for locating and destroying illegal distilleries and arresting the operators. It was therefore no surprise to me that my embezzlement case was only a minor element of the federal court docket on the day the postmaster's case was scheduled for trial.

With time on my hands before my case was to be called, I decided to observe a moonshine trial then in progress. It involved several men who had been arrested at the site of an illegal distillery. They had apparently been caught red-handed and had decided their best option was to plead guilty and throw themselves on the mercy of the court. It should be noted that, among the general populace of eastern Kentucky, moonshining was not really considered to be a dishonorable profession; the relaxed demeanor of the men standing before the judge seemed to support that contention.

Upon receiving their sentences, the men were escorted from court to begin their periods of incarceration. Immediately thereafter, a young man entered the court accompanied by his attorney. The young man had apparently been arrested by the same task force that had arrested the other men but, unlike them, he was taken into custody a half mile or so away from the site of the illegal distillery. First to testify was the county sheriff who participated in the raid coordinated by ATF agents. The sheriff was with the lead agent when they arrested the young man, and so stated in his testimony.

The next to testify was the lead ATF agent, a man in his late forties or early fifties who clearly seemed at ease in a courtroom setting. Following the usual preliminary questions having to do with his name and occupation, the prosecutor asked the agent to explain to the court how he came to arrest the young man. The agent proceeded to explain that he and the sheriff came upon the young man as he was walking about a half mile from the site of the "still," a term commonly used to denote an illegal distillery. He went on to state that they took the young man into custody and that he subsequently admitted he assisted in the operation of the still. "In fact," the agent declared, "those were his very words. He said, 'I assisted in the operation of that still.'" Apparently satisfied that the ATF agent's testimony had assured the young man's conviction, the federal prosecutor rested his case.

The defense attorney then called the young man to the witness box and, following his swearing-in, said to him, "Now, Billy, you heard the testimony of the sheriff and the government man." Billy replied, "Yes, sir." The attorney then asked, "Billy, did you assist in the operation of that still?" Again, Billy replied, "Yes, sir." Then, raising his voice several decibels, the attorney asked, "Billy, did you help those men make that moonshine?" The young man sat bolt upright in the witness box, and, in a voice one might expect from someone who had just experienced an epiphany, exclaimed "Oh, no, sir! I was just watchin' 'em; I wasn't helpin' 'em!"

Well, you could have heard a pin drop. The judge cast a withering look in the direction of the prosecutor's table where the ATF agent was sitting, and then said, in a voice brimming with anger, "It's clear to me that an error has been made here, and I look to the U. S. Attorney's office to correct it." The judge then proceeded to dismiss the charge against the young man and adjourn the court.

Although the thought of giving false testimony in any proceeding was something I never would have considered doing, the ATF agent's act of ascribing to the young man words he didn't even know the meaning of and therefore would never have used, certainly reinforced for me the wisdom of always telling the absolute truth. And while I never knew what became of that ATF agent, I strongly suspect—and sincerely hope—his federal law enforcement career ended shortly thereafter.

The Home Front: Georgia, April 1944

Pearl Wachman

It was a beautiful spring day in April at Fort Stewart in Hinesville, Georgia. Fort Stewart was a huge army war base—soldiers were coming and going. I was living there temporarily as a war bride prior to my husband being shipped out to the European war front. Savannah was a short distance away, and I decided to take the bus and explore this famous city. After all, I was a girl born, bred, and educated in New York. The South would be a new land for me to explore.

As I boarded the bus, I noticed one available seat in the rear. Of course, I sat down. The ride would take about twenty to thirty minutes, and I had some reading material to look at so that I could learn about Savannah. As I started to read, the bus driver approached me and asked me to vacate the seat. Incidentally, there were no empty seats in the bus.

I questioned the driver as to the reason for his request. The words that he uttered would never leave my memory. He said in a brisk manner, "Lady, this seat is for niggers only. You get yourself up to the front of the bus and stand if you have to until we get to Savannah." He closed, "This bus ain't moving until you do."

As shocked, angry, and disbelieving as I was, there was a question in my mind. Here we are fighting a war on two fronts: Hitler—a fascist emperor, and Hirohito—a fascist emperor, both murderers. Here in the United States, we were encountering blatant racism. Another war! "Good old Georgia" not on my mind!

Growing Up on a Farm in the Forties

Robert W. La Bree

I grew up on a farm in Guilford, Maine. Guilford is right in the center of the state, just below Moosehead Lake. It's a small town. It was even smaller in 1936 when I came on the scene. My parents bought the farm when I was about five. There were four of us kids. I had two older sisters and a brother just eleven months younger than I. It was a great place to grow up: beautiful in the spring, summer, and fall and colder than cold in the winter. Many years the snow came before Thanksgiving and stayed on the ground until after Easter. The latest snow I remember fell in June.

We had no electricity and no indoor plumbing. The house was heated with a wood furnace in the basement. We all slept on the second floor, and there was no heat up there. Sometimes we'd get a hot iron wrapped in a towel to take to bed and put down by our feet. If we needed the bathroom at night, we had a chamber pot the contents of which would be frozen in the morning. We boys often skipped using the outhouse during winter days and just "went" out the door of the shed. The snow always gave us away.

Sometimes the snow would be so high that you could not see a vehicle passing on the road unless you went to the second floor of the house. School, however, was never called off. If our road was too impassable for the school bus to get through, we had to walk up to the main road to wait for the bus. We didn't mind going to school, however, especially in the winter, because there were inside toilets there.

We were pretty much self-sustaining on the farm. We grew almost every vegetable, and Mom "put up" for the winter what we didn't eat in-season. We had a cow for our milk and butter that Mom made in the churn. We never had chickens, as Mom thought they were too messy. So, she traded some of her butter for eggs. Each year, Dad would take the cow for a visit with the neighbor's bull down the road. The resulting calf became our "beef critter," which we raised and then had slaughtered for meat to last through the year. We raised a piglet every year, and bred rabbits also, for meat.

Both my parents always held jobs outside the home, too. Dad worked at a lumber company, and Mom worked for a company that produced hardwood products. All the wood they both worked with came from Maine, and some even came from our farm. When we were old enough, my brother and I worked in our woods, cutting tress for our firewood and to sell to the hardwood products company.

When I was about seven, however, Dad was drafted and sent to Germany. That left Mom and us four kids to run the farm. Mom had to change jobs so that she would have more time at home during the day. She took a job working evenings at a woolen mill. Since she did not drive, she had to walk a mile each way through the woods to work. She walked through the woods in order to cut the distance down to one mile. Had she walked on the road, it would have been more like two and a half miles to the mill. So, rain or shine or even snow, but mostly in the dark, Mom would head out though the woods to work with flashlight in hand. I often wonder how she did that five days a week in addition to managing the farm and raising four children.

In later years, Dad, in addition to the farm and his lumber mill job, had a contract with the state of Maine to mow the roadsides in Guilford and surrounding towns. When my legs were long enough to reach the pedals on the tractor, Dad hired me for the job. I saved my money from that job, and from money I made cutting pulpwood for our neighbor who sold it to pulp mills, and bought myself a horse whose name was Tony.

I had enough money to buy Tony, but not for a saddle. I had to ride him bareback for a year until I saved enough money. I was tall enough to be able to mount Tony by vaulting up over his rump end. This worked great until one day, just as I vaulted, he decided to kick up his hind legs. I landed on his legs, which was not enjoyable for either of us. After that, I got on him by grabbing onto his mane. We'd ride through the woods and have a good old time. When we came to the brook, Tony would jump across with me on his back. It was great fun. One day, however, he decided he was not going to jump the brook and stopped dead when we reached it. Needless to say, I continued ahead jumping the brook without him. I was not too happy with Tony that day. Not much changed when I finally got the saddle. I still rode him bareback occasionally just for the fun of it.

It was an exciting life for a kid back then in the heart of Maine during the 1940s, and I'm glad I have these fond childhood memories of it to share.

(Top L to R) Kathleen Dodds, Michael Ryan
Pearl Wachman
(Seated) Mary Erwin, Roy Larson, Anne Coghlan

The Hash House

Arthur T. Erwin

Long before the Oriental Theater became the most prominent edifice in Mattapan Square, there was Andersen's Theater. Fondly called "The Hash House" by its hordes of faithful partisans—none of whom had the faintest notion of when or why it was so named. However, it was always held in deep reverence by its legion of patrons.

Be that as it may, it had the distinction of being the nearest movie theater to Milton that could provide both young and old with the marvels of Hollywood magic. And did it ever! Today, were we to use this generation's speech, we would describe it as "cool" or "awesome" or truly the "in" place to be. It was a place you enjoyed being with your friends, and you were happy all the time you were there.

Saturday was the domain of the youngsters and teenagers. On that day, the ticket office opened at 12:30. The program started at 1:00 PM and lasted until 5:00 PM. It was not at all unusual to find the house filled to capacity fifteen minutes after the doors opened. One must consider the fact that going to a Saturday matinee in those days wasn't just an event, it was a weekend ritual—part of the passage from youth to adulthood.

A typical matinee would include a Pathe newsreel; a comedy; the first of two full-length movies; and a chapter from an ongoing serial. And after intermission: a preview of coming attractions, and the main feature, another full-length movie. All this for the magnificent sum of ten cents!

Ushers were always on duty to both assist patrons and try to keep order. They were armed with flashlights not only to locate seats for latecomers but also to search out any overzealous patron who might be overcome with enthusiasm. A dire warning of eviction would, as a rule, have the desired effect, and the offender suddenly became mute.

Once the lights dimmed, an automatic blanket of silence cloaked the audience and remained in place until intermission. For the most obvious of reasons, most adults were apt to be more selective when choosing to attend performances.

Adult audiences received the gift of free dinnerware. The dishes were a benevolence to the adults for their patronage. Obviously, this did not apply to the Saturday matinee, since at least a few of the dishes would likely be transformed into lethal missiles.

The movie menu for the week was divided into thirds. New features every Sunday, Tuesday, and Friday. The strategy was that on weekends the juveniles were presented with action, adventure, mystery, horror, and western films while the remainder of the week the menu catered to the adults who were more prone to dramas, musicals, and light comedy.

To entice the audiences, their appetites were abundantly whetted by a seemingly endless string of coming attractions. In this ploy, small snippets of the coming films were tantalizingly shown—just enough to activate the most urbane of imaginations. Ergo, the patrons had a whole week to look forward to seeing the new films.

As a result, legions of youth and adults wended their way to Andersen's Theater over the years. It was a part of growing up for some, and a chance to be entertained and educated for many others. The Hash House now stands vacant in Mattapan Square. For a while, it was converted into a United States post office, but that was many years ago.

The Hash House did give birth to a bit of local folklore. Any time you went there, you didn't go to the "movies," you went to the "show." Conversely, when one later attended the Oriental Theater, you were going to the movies. But that's another story for another day.

Cunningham Park in Winter

Mary Erwin

A fond memory of my younger days was going to the winter sports held at Cunningham Park. The Cunningham family donated the land to Milton residents strictly for recreational purposes, and the children of Milton took full advantage of it.

In the winter, the swimming pool was turned into a hockey rink, one of the ponds into a general skating rink, and in between the two was the toboggan slide. In between the skating and the slide was a wooden bridge to change from one event to the other. My favorite part of the winter activities was riding the toboggan slide in the nighttime. There were lights illuminating both the skating and the slide. My evening would begin by paying twenty-five cents to rent the toboggan for a priceless experience with my friends.

After you got your toboggan, you and your excitement walked toward the start of the slide located atop the hill between the swimming pool, now hockey rink, and the large pond, now a skating rink. As you walked toward the top, you would first see the flames from the potbelly stove set up for the park attendants to stay warm. Just beyond the stove, you saw the line of children waiting their turn on the slide. The ages ranged from twelve to eighteen.

There were two tracks to guide the toboggans and its passengers on the exhilarating ride into the field at the bottom. The attendants would arrange for the loving riders to be snug in the toboggan to ensure a safe travel down the hill. After securing the anxious riders, they would lift the chute and off we would go, laughing and screaming as we came to a slow stop well into the field. My friends would say that we were racing next to each other as we went down the hill. Although you had no control over the speed or track of the toboggan, whoever won took ultimate credit in beating the other.

Once stopped, we took a deep breath and would bounce right back up to quickly get back up the hill for another run. We were pretty tired pups at the end of the evening, but it was worth it. What fun we did have!! It was a place to meet my friends and have some innocent fun all together.

Cunningham Park was the most popular place to be at night on the weekends or during school vacations. It holds many, many happy memories for me.

School for Brides

Francine Weistrop

No one told me that getting married meant learning how to cook, clean, entertain friends and, in addition, complete college, student teach, learn how to write a check, make grocery lists, and do all the chores that adults did. I was, after all, nineteen years old, had never lived on my own, and had few responsibilities except for making good grades.

Suddenly, I had to be a grown-up before I had any inkling of what that meant. I watched my mother effortlessly do all the chores, cook three meals a day, and have guests for dinner. I didn't have any concern that my time would come to do that, and I certainly had no inkling that I would have to take on the additional responsibility of being a rabbi's wife.

My husband entered the seminary at the end of the summer of our wedding. His responsibilities were scholarly: study, take oral and written exams, learn all the texts that would give him the ability to preach, teach, counsel, and be available for all life events of his future congregation. He had classmates with whom to compare notes, and he had professors to imbue him with knowledge. It was not easy, but it was designed so that he knew what was his to learn.

While I was learning how to not burn the dinner and get homework done, an invitation arrived that made the earlier tasks seem like child's play. Two of the wives of the seminary faculty invited those of us who were married or engaged to the new students to a series of meetings at their homes. I thought that was a very hospitable thing to do, and I looked forward to socializing with my peers and meeting the wives of the much admired faculty.

But it was not that simple. There was a curriculum at these gatherings. We were in training to be good rabbis' wives. We had no idea what that meant but we learned very soon.

On the assumption that most of us had led sheltered social lives compared to what it would be out in the congregational world, we were led through a series of lessons on how to do the right thing in all of our challenges. I will try to summon up what I remember being taught. They divided our lessons into categories; so will I.

Our home: In preparation for the world we were entering, we were given these rules (they called them guidelines, but we knew better): By seven thirty every morning our home needed to be immaculate; beds made, dishes done, laundry not visible, silver polished, ourselves polished, our husbands sent off with crisply ironed shirts into a spotless car. The reason for this early deadline was that one never knew when a congregant might ring the doorbell, and we needed to be ever ready.

Our children: No matter how many or how old, our children must be spotless at all times, well behaved, and friendly. No matter if they were at an age when children liked to take off their shoes and run around the yard, rabbis' children did not run around the yard without shoes. Their table manners were to be impeccable, and their voices subdued.

We knew we could not produce or train such perfect children; we were terrified that the entire town would talk about a child with a recent peanut butter stain on his or her shirt or hair with too many cowlicks to keep neat.

Ourselves: We were to wear quiet colors, keep ourselves as demure as possible, no makeup, no pants, even when on a trip to the supermarket. Our clothing was to be fashionable but never look as though we spent a lot of money on such frivolities.

If we had gone to college, as most of us had, our idea of a career was quickly nipped in the bud. We could teach at the temple, we were to be ready to entertain small groups and large, but bringing in a paycheck would reflect badly on our husbands.

We needed to be prepared to answer questions posed by our congregants on matters rabbinical, but our answers had to agree with our husbands' opinions. We were to be the *Stepford Wives* of the rabbinical school.

Our social responsibilities: At the end of each evening, our hostess moved us into the dining room where we were treated to a perfect model of what we were to be expected to do in four years.

The table was beautifully set with the silver tea set, the desserts were lovely to behold and home baked, there was a beautiful centerpiece, magnificent china, and all the things it would take us years to accumulate. But at least we knew what the role models were to be. And when we later spoke among ourselves, we all knew in advance that we would be failures.

It was far too late to change our futures. We had no choice but to prepare for this life. We invited each other for social evenings. We served on pottery with stainless-steel flatware, we had no money for flowers, but we did learn to cook and bake. It was fun because it was with friends and no one was judging us. But the fear remained.

Finally, I decided to share with my husband how these evenings were conducted and how fearful I was that I would never be as good as these two model wives. I wish I had mentioned it earlier because his response cleared away all the clouds.

"You just have to be yourself and do what is right for you, just as they are doing what is right for them."

And I did.

Horrible, Earth-Shattering, Not Me!

Virginia L. Coghlan

On Good Friday, April 1, 2009, I was undergoing a yearly mammogram at Newton Wellesley Hospital. For years, the procedure was dreaded, but the outcomes were always fine. However, this past year, the outcome was not what any woman wants to hear: "There is an apparent question of cells that do not look favorable."

Now I am in shock mode. Stuck with unfamiliar words, I reacted with, "This is just a false scare, a mistake." Yet a few days later, it was confirmed that I had breast cancer and required surgery. Later, a second cancerous breast was discovered, and now I was facing double surgery followed by intense radiation for eight and a half weeks.

But my ordeal is really the story of fabulous individuals who helped me travel through this nightmare. Without them, there would be no story.

Who to select and honor? There are so many unique, unselfish individuals. I start with my sister, Helen Kiddy, my roommate, who contacted all the top medical personnel. These caring professionals helped me begin the necessary living process.

This has been an emotional roller-coaster ride for me as I am now in recovery. Reflecting back is precious, tearful, and grateful. However, two women at Fuller Village win double billing. Judy Ward, my guardian angel, coupled with Nancy Kearns, brought with them their extraordinary strength and thoughtfulness.

Daily, several moments each day, both Judy and Nancy connected with me, brought me good wishes, homemade food, flowers, and most importantly their outstanding personal insights. There is not a word, to date, that can really express my heartfelt appreciation. They will always own a piece of my heart. Without these two special women, my trip would have been a morose journey.

The Fuller well-wishers who supplied endless verbal greetings and hordes of get well cards were amazing. Finding bags of thoughtful, delicious surprises at my door helped me appreciate the element of caring and support. Blossom Glassman, Mary Keating, Anna Donoghue, Bea Seidman, Tom and Claire Martin; the Crowley sisters' familiar knock at the door meant homemade blueberry muffins delicious from the oven. Jo Jackson called me, prayed for me daily. Ruth Coughlin always offered her fantastic spirit while Deborah Felton, Jean Powers, and many others offered rides and personal suggestions.

While the residents of Fuller Village and its director created a carefree life for me, I was also smothered in love and cared for by family members and lifelong school friends. "Yes, Virginia, there is a caring community." Yes, Hillary, it does take a village (Fuller) to care for its residents, a community of love with my deepest affections.

My café buddies, Dottie Gilman with her sidekick, Clara Martinelli, helped me find laughter at lunch plus an unneeded weight gain. Nadine was our cheerful, faithful servant in attendance.

Thanks also to Mary Wilkinson, Nancy Alfieri, Ruth Hannigan, Fran Bolos, Carol Jameson, Barbara Ahern, Mike and Shirley Ryan—they all know how much they mean to me. Yes, Eleanor Reidy, your smile and laughter was medicine from the gods. Mae and Tony Evangelista and Freddy and Muriel offered their wisdom. The list goes on and on, including the recovering Dooleys, Kay Gilligan, and Doris Waugh, who provided love, laughter, and wisdom.

It is endless, so full of sincerity, love, hope, and humor. Hello, Milt! When is Bill Murray paying for my Mercedes?

A POW Memoir

Herbert Colcord

I was captured by the Germans near the village of Moon-sur-Elle in the Normandy region of France on June 12, 1944, and repatriated in the Bavarian section of Germany near the Alps on April 29, 1945. During my eleven months as a prisoner of war (POW), I was constantly being moved—on foot, in trucks, or in rail boxcars—ultimately traveling about 1,300 miles. After an initial stop at a makeshift camp in France, I traveled for about three months, moving from north to south in Germany with stops at Stalag 12A in Limburg, Stalag 12D in Trier, Stalag 7A in Moosburg, and Stalag 7B in Memmingen. After September 1944, I spent most of my time in smaller forced-labor camps operated out of Stalags 7A and 7B. These work camps, known as *Arbeitskommando* or ARB-KDO, included ARB-KDO 659B in Wasserburg, ARB-KDO 657B in Gunzburg, and ARB-KDO 653B in Augsburg, where I stayed for about six months.

Within a few days of my capture, I found myself as a lone prisoner traveling with a German convoy. To avoid Allied air forces patrols, the convoy only drove at night. One German soldier was assigned to guard me. During this time, I learned the German army was somewhat disarrayed. For example, we were moving at night to avoid airplane attacks, but some of the trucks had their lights on. This was not very smart. As we moved under the cover of darkness, I could hear a squadron of English Mosquito bombers overhead. The Mosquito bomber was the only low-level night bomber at that time, and this squadron seemed to know the general location of our convoy. They dropped a large number of flares in an attempt to locate us. Fortunately, they never did find us or I probably would not be here today.

Another close call involving Allied planes happened while I was traveling by rail in a boxcar. I remember "celebrating" my nineteenth birthday (July 9) around this time. During one of its many stops, our train parked under a bridge. Allied planes bombed the bridge, but it was a long train and only a few cars were under it. Fortunately none of the cars were hit.

At one point, not long after I was captured, I was in a temporary camp with several hundred paratroopers from the 82nd Airborne Division. Something unusual, funny, but very dangerous, took place there. One of the prisoners had to urinate and chose a bathroom of convenience—out the second-story window. At that moment a German colonel walked by and was showered with urine. As you might expect, he was not very happy. Fortunately, he cooled off after berating us in German for about ten minutes.

My first opportunity to write a letter home was on June 27, 1944, in Stalag 12A. My mother saved the letter for me. My next memory was at Stalag 12D where I had my picture taken. This was about August 20, 1944. Just after the war ended, another soldier came across my POW record and photograph. He mailed the record to my home in North Quincy, Massachusetts, along with this note:

To whom it may concern: Found this prisoner-of-war record in the files of a German office. If Herbert is alive, which I hope he is, this would make a good souvenir for him to keep. Seeing that I live only a short distance from you, this card came to my attention. I am from Winthrop, Mass., just across the bay. If you receive this card, please write and let me know or write to Mrs. Ruth Glover, 43 Lewis Ave., Winthrop, 52, Mass. From a poor soldier in this here country waiting to go home ... PFC Edwin Glover, May 19, 1945, Memmingen, Germany.

My POW record and Private Glover's letter are among my most prized possessions.

Our boxcar arrived at camp 653B in Augsburg during November of 1944, and we stayed in that city until April of 1945. This was by far the longest amount of time we were in one place. Life here was a series of forced-work details. The work involved salvaging slates from the roofs of bombed-out buildings. This was dangerous work because the roofs were not stable. Occasionally, we were on work details when Allied bombers flew overhead. They were a constant threat because our pilots had no way of knowing we were on the ground. The Germans devised a code to indicate the level of alert—one siren meant planes over Germany, two sirens meant they were coming our way, three sirens meant they were overhead and the guards would move us to a bomb shelter. On occasion, German anti-aircraft guns would shoot down our planes.

While I was in Augsburg, some of our soldiers devised an escape plan. Two of them thought they had a pretty good chance of escaping. One spoke perfect German, and the other spoke perfect French. But that would only help them after the escape. First, we had to cover their absence. The guards counted us every night, so we devised a somewhat elaborate scheme to make the count include the two soldiers who had escaped. Everyone in our barracks was involved. The plan was successfully executed, but the two soldiers were recaptured within ten hours. Fortunately, their punishment was only one day in solitary confinement.

One day, when we were not on a work detail, the guards herded us into a bomb shelter. This was unusual. After a short time, we heard airplanes. Soon their sound became louder. As the sound increased, four or five bombs landed right on top of us, and the bunker began to cave in. Then the bombs stopped, and the planes flew off. After assuring ourselves that the planes were no longer a threat, we emerged from the shelter and were met by a shocking sight. The entire complex was in flames, and shortly thereafter it burned to the ground. Somehow the guards knew about this attack beforehand, and they actually saved our lives. I suspect the target of the bombers was a nearby Messerschmitt buzz-bomb factory. I hope it suffered the same fate as our work camp.

We were then moved to another camp in Augsburg and remained there until the middle of April. Here I clearly remember watching a one-hour bombing of the Augsburg railroad station. We were on a hill several miles away. Five minutes after the bombing ended, the German trains were running again.

The Germans moved us out of Augsburg sometime toward the end of April. We started moving as a loose-knit marching unit. During this time, a French observation plane followed us. As we approached a small German town near the Bavarian Alps, an Allied advanced unit of African-American soldiers, part of General George S. Patton's Third Army, started to fire rounds into the town. Some of the German guards returned fire, but then quickly surrendered. We were now free. My official release to Allied control was on April 29, 1945.

I was flown from Germany to France, first to Rheims and then to Le Havre, before shipping off to New York City, where I arrived on May 15, 1945. I was given leave to go home until about June 15 and then went to Lake Placid, New York, for a month of recuperation. I was still in the army. At the beginning of August, I was sent to Fort Ord on Monterrey Bay in California for four months and received my sergeant stripes. On December 7, 1945, I was discharged and gratefully returned home for good. I arrived home about December 15. It was good to be home, but two pieces of sad news were waiting for me: (1) John Spurr, who landed with me on Omaha Beach and who was wounded when the Germans captured us, had died a few weeks later on June 29, 1944; his body was brought back to the United States, and I attended his funeral in Plymouth, and (2) my dog also died while I was a POW.

After arriving home, I discovered my parents learned I was missing in action (MIA) on July 30, 1944, but did not know I was still alive until two months later. My mother fainted when she was told I was MIA, and my father lit a candle every day and prayed at a chapel in Boston. The stress of "not knowing" even affected the mailman. When my parents' letters to me were returned, he simply couldn't handle the deliveries. Finally, my parents' prayers were answered in October when the government confirmed I was a POW in Germany. *The Patriot Ledger* published the news on October 18, 1944.

Let me tell you about life in a boxcar. Each car contained about forty men. In the center of the car was a big barrel that was our toilet. All of us tried to distance ourselves from it for obvious reasons. The Germans did not feed us much, so there was a minimum of solid waste; most of it was urine. There were no windows in the car, and it was summer, so the smell was overwhelming. There were two slits up high where only the taller men could see out. While on the train, we received one small bowl of soup each day if we were lucky. Later, when we were in a permanent camp, we received bread with the soup. The train would stop occasionally to empty the toilet and take on water. The water was usually dirty, but we drank it anyway. We were not allowed out of the boxcar except to empty the toilet. I would never want to repeat this experience. I will never forget it, but will forever be grateful to God for helping me to survive it.

My life in a POW camp was similar to time spent in a boxcar. Some of the things that we take for granted, such as brushing our teeth or having a normal bowel movement, just didn't happen. Food was scarce and personal supplies non-existent. When it was available, food consisted of dark bread, soup, and water once a day. We never had a chance to shower or wash our hair. We never had a chance to drink a glass of clean water. All of our clothes, including our socks and underwear, were never washed. We wore what we had on when we were captured. We could not cut our nails or our hair. Most of us had lice. Gratefully, we were not physically abused. The abuse was emotional. There was the constant threat of air raids. We did have some limited health care, but not nearly enough. During my time as a POW, I lost about sixty pounds. I weighed 183 pounds when we crossed the English Channel and 120 pounds when we were liberated. My normal weight was 140 pounds, but the army's doughnuts and God's good grace had provided me with extra weight that would serve me well through my nearly eleven months of captivity.

A Rare Comic Experience from World War II

Hy Rossen

Picture a small hospital with a big job: to care for hundreds of U.S. military personnel, from privates to generals, attached to the Supreme Headquarters of the Allied Expeditionary Force in Paris. Then picture the building: a large "incoming" office with a long corridor leading to ten different treatment rooms. My office, eye care, was across the corridor from nose and throat care. I worked in both offices.

All patients, from privates to generals, routinely obtained entrance papers at the incoming office and then waited to be called to a treatment room. One exception was a very haughty colonel whose sinus problems brought him in only occasionally. He would stride right into the "nose and throat" room and go directly to the treatment chair. He would then glare at the nose and throat doctor, Captain Watson, and the patient in the chair and declare: "I have an appointment at a top staff meeting and need rush care." The patient and Captain Watson would invariably yield to his rank and cede the treatment chair, whereupon the colonel would get his "rush care."

One day, I saw the colonel marching down the corridor toward the "nose and throat" room. Lo and behold, he had been promoted and now strutted the one-star uniform of a brigadier general. He stomped proudly up to the treatment chair but then stopped and jumped back. Sitting in the treatment chair, being treated by Captain Watson, was a two-star general!

My Spiritual Journey

Lillian Scherban

My parents came from Austria, and their religious heritage was Ukrainian. My father came from landed gentry, and my mother had no schooling until she went to get her U.S. citizenship at forty-two years of age. The house we lived in was on the mainline trolley in order to allow my father to make it to work as a baker each night. My mother chose our particular home because she wanted to live in a house where the sunshine flooded the rooms during the day. I was born in this house. My parents had eight children and made connections to allow their children to get the best schooling available. In addition, we all received elocution lessons to allow us to speak English without an accent. Each child learned a musical instrument. I played the trumpet.

I started school at four years of age, had my first marriage proposal at fourteen, and joined a Catholic convent at nineteen. My journey into the Catholic religion was through my dancing teacher's influence. Before I met her, on alternating Sundays I would attend the Episcopal and Orthodox churches. As a senior in high school, I was selected to go to MIT to become a radar technician. I learned to build power supplies and eventually learned to install them in the B-17 bomber. After two years in that work, I went to work for Eastman Kodak.

I was always a pious kid, but when I went into the convent in September 1946, my father cried. He thought the role of nuns was to serve the clergy no matter what the religion. My mother was supportive because, when she was carrying me, she had a dream about the Blessed Mother. In her dream, the Blessed Mother was carrying lilies; hence my name became Lillian. My mother also received the following message: "The child you are bearing now shall be in the service of the

Church." But, in my mother's words, the church chosen was "the wrong church."

I became a member of the French Order, Les Filles du Saint-Esprit. The liturgy from my background was very different from the order. I could not use any slang in my language and could not speak English, only French. I felt very dependent but still called to serve the Lord and for that reason was motivated to continue by choice.

As a nun, I made a vow of poverty. It was not one of deprivation but one of dependence. In addition, I made a vow of chastity and obedience. Chastity was a vow of sexual purity, and obedience meant you go wherever you are sent and do whatever you are asked to do. For example, you could not leave a room without permission, nor could you mend stockings or throw them away without permission. While I was in the convent, my father died. I was allowed to spend time with him, and I asked whether or not he was afraid to die. His response: "With a son-in-law like I have on the other side, Jesus Christ, I have nothing to fear." He confirmed that he understood my commitment.

I left the convent in 1962. I left because in my mind my mission was accomplished. I had learned another language, and I had become an excellent public speaker. Since leaving the convent, the following are some of the experiences I have had: I was invited to lecture nationwide by the Serra International Club whose purpose was to sponsor vocations in the priesthood; I became fluent in the Russian language; I received a grant under the National Defense Education Act; I attended the University of California in San Francisco and attended Dartmouth College on a grant to study Russian; I chose to study in Africa to expand my experiences; I attended the University of Hawaii and received a master's degree in French and studied the Chinese language; I taught French at Jeanne d'Arc Academy; and I taught social studies in French in the Newton Public Schools.

My experiences in the convent made me the woman I am today.

In the Shadow of Blue Hill

Anne N. Gebhardt

Parents living in the Depression years worried about their children and how they would be affected. Most of us were hardly aware of it. Childhood to me meant family, friends, fun, exploration, and development. Even though I grew up in the Depression years, the word *depression* was not in my vocabulary. However, I was concerned for my mother, as my father had passed away, and I wondered how she would manage.

She had been looking for a new home for her little family and finally found one she liked except for two drawbacks. First, it did not have central heat and second, it had not been converted from gas light to electricity. These two features were still common in many of the stately old houses in the area.

After much consideration, my mother decided she could accept the heating system as it was: a black coal stove in the kitchen and a parlor stove that fit into the living room fireplace. The owner agreed to make the change in the lighting, and we moved into our new home.

The kitchen was large, with a big black stove that was very imposing. I had never seen one before. It was fueled by coal, which meant my sister and I would bring up a coal hod full from the basement each day and take the ashes back down. My mother had to learn how to make the fire and use the stove. She baked at least twice a week, so the oven was important to her. There was a small two-burner gas stove attached to the back for use in the summertime.

Off the side of the kitchen was a large pantry that held all of her everyday dishes, pots and pans, and foodstuffs. It also included a work area and even a window. Next was the back hall where the icebox was located. On the back wall were two large windows that overlooked the garden and commanded a view all the way to the Blue Hills. My mother loved to sit there and enjoy the views. On the sidewall were more windows and the sink. She was so happy with her new kitchen, she even decided to buy one of those new electric refrigerators. All of her friends and neighbors had to come in to see this new convenience and her new home.

The kitchen soon became the center of activity. The closeness of the family was ever present. It was where we dined, did our homework, played games, and shared our thoughts and sometimes our secrets. My mother had a small portable sewing machine, and I turned the handle while she guided the material; even some of her very good friends were invited into this special room. The end of the day was marked with Bible reading and evening prayers and then off to bed for my sister and me.

My mother's kitchen was as precious to her as an elegant parlor might have been to someone else. Her special place was by the windows looking to the hills, reminiscing or perhaps dreaming of what life might be for her daughters.

What wonder that one day I would live on the side of Blue Hill next to the reservation land and eventually move to a place called Fuller Village in the shadow of Blue Hill.

A Significant Life-Changing Event

Gwen Senger

The day my son was diagnosed with paranoid schizophrenia was the day my whole world changed. It brought me closer to God and made me more sympathetic to those who could not help themselves.

I never knew about mental illness until my son, Wayne, had to leave junior high school in a small town in New Hampshire. He was running around and saying people were trying to kill him. He was committed to a New Hampshire mental hospital and given heavy medication. I felt I would faint when I saw him. The conditions in a mental hospital in the 1960s were terrible. The employees did the best they could with their lack of knowledge and without the improvements we now see.

A short time after that, we moved back to my childhood home in North Quincy with the prospect of my son being transferred to a mental facility in the Boston area. In the meantime, my husband had lost his job, as did many others in the economic downturn. After six months, he found another job in the Boston area in the technical art field. Our daughter, Brenda, had to adjust to the fifth grade in Quincy. Two years later, she enrolled in the Lexington Christian Academy and traveled to classes each day on the train.

Wayne was at home at times, and we tried to rehabilitate him. Unfortunately, the professional field told us it was the fault of the parents that Wayne was acting the way he did. At that time, medicine to control behavior was just starting to be used. Sometimes Wayne was so medicated, we would have to carry him. Now, forty years later, many mentally ill patients are living productive lives out of the hospital. So much has been accomplished for housing and employment for them.

After Chapter 766 was enacted in Massachusetts, help was offered to those in school until they reached the age of twenty-two. After that, there was nothing. A psychiatric nurse from Medfield State Hospital formed a group of eight parents to discuss their problems. We met in a local church. We first named the group "Citizens Organization Assisting Mental Patients." Later we met at the Quincy Mental Health Center. I was president of this organization for thirteen years and enjoyed working with the unusually dedicated and loyal officers and their families. This was the first group in the state to form. We later became the "South Shore Alliance for the Mentally Ill," which covered Milton, Quincy, and Randolph.

There was also a group formed called the Coastal Alliance, which covered Weymouth, Hull, Hingham, Norwell, and Braintree. We would meet together at the Quincy Mental Health Center. Eventually, other alliances throughout the state were formed and became the "Massachusetts Alliance for the Mentally Ill." A National Alliance for the Mentally Ill was formed; all three organizations are still in existence. The South Shore group and the Coastal Alliance continue to meet together at the Quincy Medical Health Center and still are working on issues of more private and government help.

We also address the need for more education regarding mental illness. We strive to eliminate the stigma of mental illness and to provide quality living for those afflicted. We have psychiatrists and other professionals in the mental health field come to speak to our group. Patients—now called consumers—have their own group. The CAUSE program, which has been very successful, helps them in continuing their education in local colleges and in finding jobs.

One traumatic incident in my trying to help was going to the State House in Boston. I spoke to our representatives at the Gardner Auditorium and told them about why it was so important to keep the South Shore Mental Health Center open for crisis issues, transportation issues, and programs to prevent more catastrophes. I had never been a speaker and was rather quiet and shy until I became a crusader for the mentally ill.

I was on the board of the Quincy Medical Health Center and also on the Friends of Medfield Board and active in the Massachusetts Alliance after it was formed. Each year at Christmas, our group brought food to the South Shore Unit at Medfield State Hospital. This homemade food (including desserts!) was made by the families, and beverages were supplied by the Copeland family in Milton. We brought gifts for each consumer, which our "Santa" distributed. Patients and families enjoyed the music that we provided.

Because of the money cutbacks, Medfield State Hospital and the sixty-day in-patient unit at Quincy Medical Health Center are no longer functioning. Because of the availability of better medications, consumers are now living in group homes and other facilities nearer their loved ones. There is still a need for hospitals to stay open for those who are severely ill and cannot function outside. This is a great hardship for those who must commute long distances to see their loved ones. We are thankful for such good friends who helped relieve us at times; caring for Wayne exhausted us both mentally and physically. With the grace of God, however, we did get through it.

In 1992, because many hospitals were closing, Medfield Hospital took in some more consumers from another hospital. Wayne, who was doing well mentally, was ready to go to a halfway house and work program. Unfortunately, he was neglected and misdiagnosed as having bronchitis that, in fact, was really lung cancer. He was spitting up blood; a patient told an aide and Wayne was sent to Natick Hospital. He died in five days, much to the surprise of everyone. His life from the age of fourteen to thirty-four years was one of trying so hard, but now he had peace.

I felt I had lost my real son when the schizophrenia disease took him at the age of fourteen. It was so difficult to let go and not have him home, but one can do only so much and then has to let go. This is when I decided to do all I could to help those with the disease. But at the age of eighty, I'm doing much less although I still do what I can. My husband is doing the same. We are so grateful we have a lovely daughter and son-in-law and two lovely grandchildren, all of whom are doing well.

My Family and Friends Are My Estate

Kathleen M. Dodds

Today as I tore a page from my calendar, I noticed a quote by Emily Dickinson, "my friends are my estate," and it started me thinking of the many relatives, friends, and acquaintances who were part of my life. Each of them contributed to my growing into me.

My Mother, Henrietta Scherer: In addition to all those character building values—style and grace. Henrietta was always on the cutting edge of fashion. As a young adult, she worked in a shoe factory. Her foot just happened to be sample size, so on paydays, it was shoes, not dollar bills that went home.

My dad, Joe Scherer: Sociability. He loved to entertain people by telling a good story whether true or not. He could also talk a dog off a meat wagon, and so can I.

My Aunt, Irene Lanchester: Faith. By example, she taught me that all things can be endured.

Jim Lordan, my work mentor: Self-confidence. Jim's motto was "no one can screw things up so badly that I can't fix it." And you know what? It was true.

Helen Marguardt: Class. Helen educated me in proper dining etiquette by telling me "always start from the outside in, and you'll never commit a faux pas. And when in doubt, start slowly and observe others."

Noreen Rowley: Patience. After all, she puts up with me, and we are still good and close friends.

Judy Peters: The true meaning of friendship, Loyalty. A quality I think...no, I know, I possess.

My daughter, Denise Dodds: Tenacity. Through good times and bad, she keeps herself focused on her goal and ultimately achieves it.

Dominic Minnelli: Humor. He taught me to laugh at myself.

Barbara MacNeil: Dance. I'm a good dancer today because of her, but I sometimes have problems with the jitterbug. She was left-handed, and so it goes.

Jo Connors: Empathy. Through her, I have become more tolerant and understanding of people.

Ruth Fernald: Conviviality. After high school graduation, Ruth went her way and I went mine; thirty-eight years later, Ruth opened her home, family, and heart and welcomed me in. This is a trait that I much admire.

Mary Neville: Altruism. Mary puts other people first. She is always concerned for the welfare of others. She inspires me to be a little less selfish in my own life.

My brothers, Bill and John Scherer: Reconciliation. Through them, I learned that it is better to put hurt and anger aside and get on with life. Something I still work on.

Rosemary Ahern: Gentility. From Rosemary, I am learning what being a class act is all about. Hopefully, it's not too late in life to rub off on me.

And to the many other friends—too many to mention—who have contributed, and some who are still contributing to my growing process, I would like you to know that I am grateful.

What Happened?

Sharon Becker La Bree

When I was eighteen years old and in college, I fell in love with a twenty-year-old fellow in my anatomy and physiology class. He was a sophomore physical education major, and I was a freshman nursing student. Two weeks after I graduated, we married. We had three beautiful children, whom we raised to be wonderful giving adults. We even had two grandchildren before he left me.

When I was fifty-eight years old and an assistant director of nursing at a Connecticut hospital, my world turned upside down. My job was being redesigned and would no longer be available to me. I had the option of another position within the hospital or a generous separation package. It was a difficult time in my life and a difficult decision about which I prayed very hard for direction. I felt very strongly that I was being led by the Lord to leave the familiar, take the package, and...and what? I knew that I would probably have to find another job, somewhere, when the package ran out. But I cared for my elderly parents in my home with the help of my husband and wonderful nursing assistants. I thought this time would give me the opportunity to spend quality time with my parents in their remaining days, so I took the package.

On Friday November 30, 2000, I left the job I had held for twenty-one years and the hospital where I had worked for thirty-three years. That night, my husband appeared with a bouquet of flowers and a bottle of champagne and a big smile to welcome in this new time in our lives. The next day he died. It was a sudden death. It came out of the blue! He had not been sick. The call came from my pastor. My husband had been taken to the hospital. A possible stroke, I was told. I went immediately. He was in cardiac arrest when I arrived. He was only sixty years old. He was dead.

To add to the drama of the day, my youngest daughter and her two young sons, three and four years old, had driven for nine hours from Virginia that day to help me celebrate my new beginnings. She knew that leaving my job was bittersweet but had been firm in insisting that, if I felt led to leave, I had no choice but to leave. She was also our only child who my husband had the opportunity to actually see being born. As a result, she always held a special place in his heart. And, he could do no wrong in her eyes. I had to tell her. How could I tell her?

But God is good. My next-door neighbor was a medical examiner for the state of Connecticut. I called him from the hospital. He was home. I told him Bob Becker had died. He said he and his wife would come for me. He accompanied me as I told my daughter. His wife took the little boys to her house to play. He and my daughter held me while I told my parents. I was in shock. But, I think my parents were way beyond shock. He had been like a son to them. Neither of us had any brothers or sisters and had been best friends for forty years and married for thirty-six. He practically lived at my house during college. He was like their son for forty years. They grieved for him and for me. What would happen to me now? My husband was dead. They were dying. They were inconsolable. They could not understand why he was taken and they, who were old and ill, were not.

My daughter called her sister and brother. My oldest daughter was at work in a hospital in Massachusetts. She left her patients to other nurses. My son lived in Maine. He and his wife had recently suffered an uncompleted pregnancy and were still very fragile. And they all were coming home to Connecticut to me, to him, to say good-bye.

Each of my three children spoke at the funeral mass for their father. They told of the man who had been so important in their lives. How were they ever able to do that? I choke up just writing this. It was such a sad time in all our lives. It was so hard to believe that it really happened, but we survived. Now, it is easier to speak of the good times in our lives: of the fun they had growing up, of camping, of their ball games that Dad always attended, of life with him and life without him.

Since Bob's death, both my parents have gone, too. Mom said he'd be saving them seats. I have moved on. I married another wonderful man also named Bob. Together we have traveled the world from Athens to Antarctica, New Zealand to Zimbabwe, Botswana to Bali, and have many places yet to go. We've moved to Massachusetts to be closer to my children. Both girls live outside of Boston now. My son is still in Maine. And I, I am here at Fuller Village making many new friends. I love both my husbands. I am happy. Life is good. My children are well. I have seven grandchildren now. But, I sit here writing this with tears running down my checks. Still trying to believe, even ten years later, that all of this really happened? It's just so different from what I would have ever anticipated.

(L to R) Brush Hill Concierge Muriel Pellegrino
Fuller Village Executive Director Deborah M. Felton
Activities Director Lisa Coover

My Father's Gift

Blossom Glassman

Some of life's best lessons are those that happen when we least expect them. These are the ones that often leave the most lasting imprint. It was in the course of one such experience that I learned one of my most valuable lessons.

In 1957, I graduated from Boston University with a master's degree in speech and language therapy. A wonderful position in the Framingham Public Schools soon followed. I would initiate and develop their first speech therapy program in the public school system with an annual salary of $3,900, an above standard starting salary at that time. I was so proud. I was so excited. I was so desperately in need of a car!

My father offered to search it out. A new car would be best, perhaps a Ford or Chevrolet. There was no further discussion. The question of financing never was broached. My father was a man who was generous and giving to his family. He took such great joy in making his loved ones happy that it was easy for me to believe he had planned this car as a graduation gift.

True to his word, he succeeded in his search, and we met at the dealership where a beautiful 1957 red and white Ford Fairlane sedan was waiting for me to inspect. I fell in love at first sight. Its sleek lines, white interior, and slim tailfins far exceeded my expectations. My heart was pounding so fast I could hardly breathe, and the tears fell while I hugged my father with a stream of thank-yous.

As he artfully negotiated with the manager, I sat quietly and apart, half listening while words about price and down payment floated about the room until the deal was finally concluded with a series of handshakes. And then we were off but not toward home. We headed east downtown and pulled into the parking lot of our bank where I guessed his funds for the down payment would be withdrawn.

Once inside, my father turned to me and patiently explained that we would be taking my war bonds from our safety deposit box and cashing them in for the down payment on the car's agreed to price of $2,000. It was important for me that I do this, he said. The time had come for me to assume adult responsibility. And it was also important for me to know that he had complete confidence in me.

I could not believe what I was hearing! Cash in my war bonds? Was it possible that he expected that I alone would be responsible for financing my car? Was it really possible that I had misjudged my father's intentions? I looked at him questioning, and he silently nodded as if to affirm my thoughts.

The return trip to the dealership was a quiet one as I tried to sort out a battle of emotions. How could I have allowed myself to be so naïve? I was overwhelmed with fear and doubt, with feelings of anxiety and uncertainty. But soon it was my father's trust that calmed my fears, and I knew he was right. It was time for me to trust in myself.

The transaction was completed. I looked at the payment books in my hand; they best represented what the word *responsibility* truly meant. And I remember thinking that my father knowingly and wisely had given me the best gift of all.

Half My Roots

Gerard J. "Jerry" Joyce

At long last, I set out to find those roots of my mother, Mary MacDougall. My wife, Marjorie, and I checked into the Margaree Lodge on the Cabot Trail in Cape Breton, Nova Scotia, Canada. Eighty years before, a sweet, sixteen-year-old Scotch-Canadian lass left the family farm in Southwest Margaree, Cape Breton, to seek her destiny in Boston, Massachusetts.

I told my story about Ma to the young lady at the desk. She took me immediately to the kitchen and introduced me to the owner, Mrs. MacIsaac, who was helping prepare the evening meal. Mrs. MacIsaac could not help me locate the MacDougall farm but suggested I see Charlie MacDonald, the postmaster, at the bottom of the hill, as he was very knowledgeable of the Margaree Valley and its people.

As the post office was closing shortly, we went at once to see Charlie MacDonald. With the little information I gave him, Charlie was stumped. He mentioned a MacDougall family with a long history, but it did not sound like my mother's family. He suggested Donald MacLellan and Fred Smith, two long-time residents of Southwest Margaree, who might be helpful.

I stayed in the post office for a while as he waited on customers and, at the same time, asked them if they knew of a MacDougall family of many years ago. Charlie and I sort of struck up a bond, and finally he suggested he would ride over to Fred Smith's with me that evening.

After dinner at the Margaree Lodge, Marjorie and I picked up Charlie MacDonald and proceeded to Fred Smith's house. Fred pointed to a field in the distance on the other side of the Margaree River and said a MacDougall family lived there many years ago. This threw Charlie way off as he was thinking about another MacDougall family. We were getting nowhere, and I began to think this was a dead end.

Then Fred mentioned something that changed the whole picture. He said the father, John MacDougall, had been chopping trees in the woods and was killed by a falling tree. This amazed me, as it was one of the few facts about my mother's family that I knew. This information was also astounding, as the death occurred about ninety years ago and Fred hardly looked sixty. Charlie explained to me later that in the winter months, the older people would pass along stories of the area to the younger ones, thus preserving the history of the locality and its people.

Fred then went in his house and brought his mother out to meet us. We talked to her in Gaelic, the same as I recall my mother did talking to her sisters and friends from "down east." "Herring-chokers" Pa used to call them, especially when he was angry or upset, which was not infrequent.

At first, Fred's mother was very suspicious of me, wanting to know my interest in the property. Thinking I was interested in buying property, she clammed up and even acted hostile, refusing to give me any information. Charlie was able to convince her that my only interest in the property was in checking my family roots. After that, she was most hospitable and confirmed Fred's information.

Standing in his yard, Fred pointed across the valley on the other side of the river at the remains of an old barn; all that was visible was the broken-down foundation. He said my Uncle Danny had built the barn as a young man. The house had long since been destroyed.

Fred then mentioned a strange incident. "Many years ago, a man by the name of MacDougall came here for a few days. He would stand over there by that tree for hours looking across the alley at his old farm, all the time crying to himself softly." Fred said it must have been one of my uncles. I figured out it had to be my Uncle Duncan. He owned the farm for many years after he had left Cape Breton for Boston with his young brother, Danny, and their mother. The girls in the family had left for Boston years earlier.

Fred told Charlie how we could drive over there. We thanked Fred, and then Charlie took us back a mile where we made a right turn by St. Joseph's Church with the pretty cemetery in front of it. Then we took another right turn down a long dirt road on the other side of the Margaree River.

We rode for about a mile, but Charlie was unable to locate the property, so we kept riding along the dirt road by the river. Luckily, the road remained good, and eventually we came out to a main road. Charlie was mystified at being unable to locate the property or the marker of Christmas trees we knew were there. Charlie decided we should see the other long-time resident of the area, Donald MacLellan, at his farm on the same road as Fred Smith's house.

Consulting with Donald turned out to be another stroke of good luck. Donald, who later said he was eighty, pointed to the same land as the MacDougall farm. He said he owned the land at one time, raised Christmas trees on it, which at the time paid for his son's college education.

He remembered the name Joyce and said he had visited Ma in Boston fifty-five years ago. It was strange, but I vaguely remembered this, even though I was just a little boy at the time. He said he knew Pa as a stubborn old Irishman. He said he had had a big argument with Pa over the Jack Dempsey-Gene Tunney heavyweight title fight.

Donald pointed out to us the same remains of the barn in the distance across the picturesque valley and the clump of old Christmas trees that Charlie could not see from the dirt road. Donald said he would take me to the property. I agreed to come back to his farm about nine o'clock the next morning.

The next morning, I drove to Donald's house. He invited me in to meet his wife, daughter, and a boarder living there. His wife made me coffee and gave me homemade bread and cookies—the same homemade bread I remember my mother making. Store bread was considered inferior bread by my brothers and sisters, thanks to my mother.

Donald gave me some boots to wear as he said the fields would be wet and muddy. We took the same dirt road by the church that ran on the other side of the river. Donald said the road was treacherous in the winter as parts of it did not get the sun, and it was easy to slide into the river.

We stopped when we got to MacFarland's farm, which was next to Ma's. The path from the road to the MacFarland property was the only way to get on and off Ma's property. It was a long hike up what had been a good wide path at one time. It had been dug up badly by the heavy equipment used to bring down logs from the mountaintop of MacFarland's property. This property was also deserted. The house had burned to the ground several years ago since the volunteer firemen had been unable to get water up to the fire. Grass and weeds had overgrown the area, so that you could not tell there had once been a house there.

Trudging up the steep path, Donald expected me to be winded, as he thought of me as a soft city fellow. Perhaps I should have chided him, as he was well aware of the fact that at least half of my roots were as strong as his roots. Halfway up the path, Donald showed me the remains of what once had been a path to the MacDougall farm, the one used to get on and off their property. We climbed up high enough to be on a level with the remainder of the MacFarland house. Then we crossed over the wet, muddy fields to Ma's old farm. I was glad I had boots on! Quite a bit of water was running down from the mountaintop. Donald said the rain had been excessive this year. This water was probably the same water Ma's family had used.

We came upon the rubble of Ma's old home. A little farther over were the remains of the barn built by my Uncle Duncan, according to Donald, that we had first seen from a distance on Fred Smith's farm. This property of one hundred acres was on the side of the mountain and extended over the top well on the other side. When I asked Donald the name of the mountain, he said, "We just call it the mountain." I was surprised it had no local name. I had never seen a single lot of one hundred acres, so I was impressed.

Donald said, "Your grandfather was chopping hard wood on the other side of the mountain for the family's use in winter. The hardwood burned better and was only found in the woods well on the other side. He was struck by a falling tree and was caught somehow by the tree upside down. When Isabel, his wife, came looking for him in the woods, she found him dead suspended upside down, trapped high up by the branches of the tree. Donald remarked sadly, "What an ordeal for a young wife to see."

I surveyed the rest of what was once my mother's home. The land sloped down to the Margaree River, but near the bottom, there was a drop of one hundred feet to the river road, making the land very inaccessible except through MacFarland's property to the dirt road.

This side of the hundred acres was cleared land, although none of the land was in use. Over in a corner was a clump of

Christmas trees, once cultivated, now growing wild. The top of the mountain area and all on the other side was a very heavily wooded section. Even to my urban eyes, it seemed as if it were rather bleak land to farm, which was the reason the MacDougall family came down to Boston.

Now I understand why my mother and aunts never wished to talk about the farm, as it had been a very poor, hard life. They were certainly sturdy, frugal Scots and earned everything they got the hard way.

Donald told me, "Families in those days used to salt away a barrel of fish and a barrel of meat from their own slaughtered farm animals for the winter. They also would put away potatoes and other farm crops. This provided them with food for the long, hard winter. The fuel for heat was wood from the trees on the property."

About the same time as my mother left Canada, "from across the puddle" and "the bogs of Ireland" a strong-tempered young man left his geese, cows, and squealing pigs in Claremorris, County Mayo, Ireland. Pa joined his older brothers and sisters in the mill town of Monson, Massachusetts.

Ma and Pa contributed thirteen children to the American scene, seven boys and six girls, gifted with a sturdy Scotch-Irish heritage. My mother and father, and waves and waves of other immigrants from the old country, built better than they dreamed.

Although my mother passed away in 1945, finding her birthplace shed a new perspective on my memories of her. She had courage, character, and loyalty to leave her family at the tender age of sixteen. Ma worked as a receptionist for a Dr. Bowes in the Dorchester section of Boston and dutifully sent money back to her family in Canada.

It was a wonderful thrill to see and walk on the farm my mother had called home eighty years before, to drink in and embrace her beautiful Margaree Valley and explore the picturesque Cabot Trail of Cape Breton Isle, Canada.

The Quincy Quarries

William H. Mulligan

The Quincy quarries were so much a part of my youth, the memory remains as clear as though it was just yesterday. It is the summer of 1943. Some one hundred young men are sunning and reclining on accommodating rocks surrounding the quarry. Others are swimming, jumping, or diving into the clear, cool water.

World War II is in full swing and many of the former "quarry rats" (as we were known) are in the service. Some are learning to fly aircraft so that occasionally one or more of the yellow, open-cockpit training planes would swoop down over the quarry as if to salute the current crop of quarry rats.

If someone arrived at the quarry wearing swim trunks, the trunks were soon discarded so as not to look out of place. On the quarry walls near the jumping/diving ledges were the painted first names of the artists. Thus "High Kevin" and "Low Kevin" identified two leaping or diving sites, "High Kevin" being about twenty-five feet above the water and "Low Kevin" being only about ten feet above. Other leaping-off places were named for their requirements or degree of difficulty.

A hushed sense of anticipation would surround the quarry as the word was passed that "Moose" was preparing to negotiate the "Runny." Moose was a three-hundred-pounder, who was one of only two who would attempt the Runny, which required the participant to run full-speed to the takeoff spot in order to clear the rocks that extended out from the quarry wall thirty feet down. Moose would clear the rocks by only about two feet, and the gigantic splash invariably evoked delight and applause from the onlookers.

Inevitably, the warm day ends, and it's time to leave the quarry. Those who had thirty cents could buy a large ice cream cone at The Hollow that would help ease the long walk or the hitchhiked ride back to the Blue Hills Parkway area of Milton.

The same ritual would be repeated daily throughout the summer until school began or work interfered.

Fuller Village Memoir Project Consultants
Dr. Katie Conboy and Suzette Martinez Standring

My Friend Ruth

Myrtle Ruth Flight

Ruth was a woman who has been in my life since my teenage years. She was two very distinct people: on one hand, short-fused and quick-tempered, on the other, pleasant and generous, almost to a fault. Picture this:

> A month ago she was walking in the corridor at Fuller Village, halting, bent over, and weaving back and forth. Coming in the opposite direction was another person in similar condition. Ruth handed her cane to the individual. A generous gesture with a twinkle in her eye," and the comment "Take it, you have longer to live than I." Two weeks later, she died at the age of ninety-four.

She was always a fashion picture. She had been a member of her church for sixty years, served Milton Hospital in the gift shop for twenty-seven years and 11,000 volunteered hours, and was an ombudsman for nursing home patients in the area. The students at Blue Hills Regional Vocational School loved Ruth and held a special birthday party for her each year in the culinary arts department.

In October, approximately two years ago, Ruth decided to travel to New Hampshire to view the fall foliage. She didn't tell anyone at Fuller where she was going, stopped at a consignment shop to get money owed her, and headed north. She drove over the New Hampshire state line, had lunch with a friend, and decided to return to Milton. When she got to Milton, she missed the turnoff and ended up in New York City. In New York, she went into a hotel, parked her car, and stayed for a couple of days. Her friends at Fuller missed her, and a five-state alert was put out looking for Ruth.

She called a friend at Fuller informing her she was all right and would be home in two days. Two days passed, and no Ruth. Ruth had started home, taken the wrong road, and ended up in upstate New York. Finally, her son received a telephone call from Geneva, New York. Ruth was at a 7-Eleven store in Geneva, and the clerk was concerned. Her son asked him to find a room for her for the night, and her son and grandson drove to get Ruth and the car and brought her back to Fuller. We all breathed a sigh of relief.

A few weeks later, it was snowing at night, and Ruth was returning to Fuller on 138 from church when she saw a blue light flashing behind her. She pulled over to the side of the road, and a state trooper stepped up to the car. He was questioning whether or not there was an adult driving because he could not see anyone behind the wheel—she was so short. When he questioned her, she gave him a hard time, and he refused to allow her to drive the one-half mile to Fuller. He called a tow truck, then asked Ruth if she would like a ride home. She refused.

A tow truck arrived, and the driver hooked up the car and asked Ruth if she would like a ride home. She agreed. He lifted her into the front seat of the truck and brought her back to Fuller. When they reached the front door, the driver lifted her out of the seat and proceeded to carry her upstairs to her apartment. There was a bingo game in progress, and as Ruth and the driver passed the players, she shouted out with a smile, “I’ve been pinched.”

My last story is about a night I found her needing a ride home. While I was filling the car with gas, a friend went into the variety store to purchase milk for her; she locked us out of the car.

Ruth, I don’t worry about you anymore, but I miss the spice you added to life.

The Road to Citizen of the Year

Francis P. McDermott

At the ripe old age of twenty-six, and after having completed a hitch in the navy, won a seat on the Milton Town Meeting, obtained a college degree, got a job as an insurance claims adjustor, and met and married the girl of my dreams, it appeared the course of my life was firmly set. But that was before a claims manager suggested I obtain a law degree. It made abundant sense to me, and I subsequently applied to and was accepted into the Suffolk Law School. It was the best career decision I ever made.

With eight years in the claims department and after passing the bar exam, I was invited to join the legal department at the Wausau Insurance Company. Three lawyers did workman's compensation, and I did trial work in the district and superior courts. It was a great experience and was a great foundation for my later legal life.

During this period I was elected president of the Waltham, Watertown, Weston, Newton Bar Association. I represented the bar in its dealings with the judges of the Waltham District Court. This included discussions regarding assignments of public defenders and rates of compensation, among other things. Perhaps because of this experience, I was elected on a number of occasions to the board of directors of the Middlesex County Bar Association. It was a very active bar association and was noted for its annual banquet at the Boston Park Plaza Hotel.

In 1971, two of my fellow attorneys at the Wausau Insurance Company and I decided to leave and form our own law firm. We were very fortunate in that the national legal manager continued to send us business. The firm was a success from the start.

In 1983, I decided to open up my own firm in Milton. The firm had seven lawyers and three secretaries and continued in business until 1994, when I retired. It was during this period that I was appointed as a temporary assistant attorney general, and I tried a number of cases for the Commonwealth.

While I was practicing law in Milton, the Milton Cable Company sought a license to operate in Milton. This required the approval of various town boards. I, along with others in town, was instrumental in the necessary license being issued.

While practicing in Watertown and Milton, I was appointed by the board of Bar Overseers to hear and adjudicate complaints against members of the bar. While it was an honor to receive such an appointment, it was sometimes distressing to hear the details of how some people go wrong. One could become very upset that some people would bring shame on an honorable profession. In sitting on these committees, we learned that the law was not for everyone.

On a number of occasions, I was elected as a governor of the Mass Academy of Trial Lawyers. This was and is a very active group working to insure the rights and privileges of the public. There were representatives from both the plaintiff and defendants bar.

During this period, I served as a Milton Town Meeting member for forty-five years and served on the Milton Personnel Board for twenty-five years, sixteen of them as chairman. Since the members of the board had no political ambitions, we were able to do our job in a businesslike manner and never sought publicity. During this period, the board reviewed and enacted a new system of classifying town employees (except the school department). We instituted a new system for all employees with regard to work duties and levels of compensation. The board also reviewed levels of compensation for non-union and elected officials and continuously monitored changes in cost of living in order to make annual adjustments at the annual town meeting.

I joined the Wollaston Golf Club in 1969 and was elected clerk of the corporation in 1983. I subsequently instituted a monthly newsletter called "Squanto Sez" to bring the current news of the club to the members. Golfers will appreciate that I had to include in the letter that I had scored a hole-in-one and an eagle.

In 1959, I joined the Knights of Columbus and became grand knight of the Scituate Council. Upon completion of that term, I was appointed a district deputy supreme knight. I also served as state ceremonial chairman and state parliamentarian.

In 1957, I married Dorothy Davock, a graduate of Notre Dame Academy in Roxbury and Boston State Teachers College (now the University of Massachusetts). We have six children, and I am proud to say all six have college degrees, and three have graduate degrees.

Mary Beth graduated from Anna Maria College and has a masters degree in speech pathology from Worcester State. Kathleen graduated from Boston College and Suffolk Law School. Paul graduated from Northeastern University. Patricia attended Old Dominion in Norfolk, Virginia and graduated from Aquinas Junior College. Lynne graduated from the University of Maine and has a masters in international relations from Georgetown University. Thomas graduated from Merrimack College.

I am very fortunate to have lived a long and fruitful life, but I do not think any award equals being named Milton's "Citizen of the Year" in 2001. The guidelines for selecting the Citizen of the Year state the person selected "must have contributed unselfishly of his time to promote the civic interest of the town." Alluding to those guidelines and my receipt of that year's award, a local newspaper article opined, "Mr. McDermott has more than satisfied this guideline."

Fifty Years Ago

A 1995 poem by Holocaust Survivor Kurt Ladner
In Remembrance of his Liberation from Dachau
April 30, 1945

In Dachau, freezing cold, ice, and snow,
where I suffered ...fifty years ago.

Hard labor, sickness, exposed to winds that blow,
I was near death...fifty years ago.

Vicious SS guards tormenting, grinning from head to toe,
watching me shiver...fifty years ago.

Dysentery, typhus, and lice that seem to grow,
drained my blood...fifty years ago.

Nothing to eat, quarantined, lost everyone I know,
to the "Final Solution"...fifty years ago.

The Allied Forces came and beat their foe,
I was liberated...fifty years ago.

Alone, my family gone, recovery very slow,
I started a new life...fifty years ago.

These sad memories, thoughts that come and go,
of terrible years...fifty years ago.

But all must deal with "Life" however high or low,
with hope, there will be no repetition...of fifty years ago.

~

January 27 is Holocaust Remembrance Day. On that date in 1945, the Russian army liberated Auschwitz. The liberation of all concentration camps was completed in April of that year.

Having suffered for three years in four different camps—Terezin, Auschwitz, Birkenau, and Dachau—it is very painful for me to remember. Yet there are those who cruelly declare the Holocaust never happened.

Poetic justice would have those deniers experience what I, along with millions of other innocents, endured. But that terrible time must never be repeated.

The Holocaust is very well documented in pictures, testimony, and witnesses. General Eisenhower and many other world leaders, past and present, have asked that this tragic chapter never disappear from the public consciousness.

Today, my wife, Betty, and I live in Fuller Village among good and caring neighbors, and we look forward to seeing a happy old age.

The Blizzard of 1978

Edith Yoffa

It started to snow on Monday, February 6. The roads were plowed through the night, so my husband, Yana, and I went off to work Tuesday morning. As the morning progressed, so did the intensity of the snow and wind, so much so that we were allowed to leave work well before noon. I lived only a few miles from my workplace, so it was not too long a ride home. Yana, on the other hand, worked in Woburn, approximately a forty-minute drive.

I spoke to Yana a few times during the next few hours urging him to leave work. He usually traveled home on Route 128 to the Milton exit onto Route 138, then Neponset Valley Parkway to Truman Highway where we lived. During our final conversation of the afternoon, about 2:30 PM, Yana said he was leaving shortly and would travel through Boston. I was upset that he was leaving so late as the snow was accumulating rather quickly and blowing more forcefully.

The weather reports were not too encouraging. The plows were out, but the winds were gusting with the snow swirling. I kept going from window to window checking the highway, which by the way, is a four-lane divided road under the jurisdiction of the state. There were still some cars getting through. Now it was getting dark. The news reported that cars were getting stuck on Route 128, but I hadn't heard too much about the expressway having problems. About eight or nine o'clock, I decided to call the highway department to check if there were problems through the city from the North Shore on the expressway and was told the cars were getting through. They told me not to worry. "Your husband probably stopped somewhere for a beer." So, I gave the situation some thought and decided Yana was on Route 128 after all. It was a worrisome night.

Sometime the next morning the phone rang; it was Yana and he was safe—at Mary Hardigan's Restaurant on Route 1A in Dedham. Early that morning, a policeman came along the highway—it had stopped snowing—and advised everyone stranded in the area to leave their keys in the ignition and climb up a nearby steep hill, bringing them to the restaurant. There were other restaurants as well as the Holiday Inn and a movie complex where other people were directed to go.

At Mary Hardigan's, they were given hot coffee. Everyone was chilled to the bone from their overnight ordeal. Then they stood in line at the pay phone to call home—just a few words to say where they were and that they were safe. They would all have the opportunity to call back with more details after the initial calls were made; there were no cell phones in 1978.

I don't recall what time that day Yana called again, but it certainly was a relief to receive that second call to tell me what took place after he could go no further. There was at first a little camaraderie with the few people in the cars close by. They would clean the snow away from the exhaust pipes to make sure they would be okay while running the car for a little warmth. With the wind still gusting and the snow still falling, Yana's head and coat were getting wet.

In his wagon, there was a knitted hat I had purchased at Filene's that he was going to return for me. He removed it from the box and put it on. It felt especially good, as he didn't have much hair for warmth. He was an industrial hardware salesman and drove a station wagon. Sometime he would make a delivery when calling on a customer. In the car were a number of cartons, plus he had lined the bottom of the wagon with pieces of corrugated cartons. He took some of the pieces and layered them under his coat to keep dryer when going out into the storm.

Everyone had to stay at the restaurant that night, as there was no way to get home. They were fed, and it was warm. How fortunate to be there. The streets and highways had to be plowed. Governor Michael Dukakis declared a "no travel" edict for the week on state roads except for essential travel and emergencies.

Meanwhile, back at "1064"—I was snowed in; I couldn't open my side door. The snow had drifted half way up. Also the dining room windows were inaccessible. Likewise, I could neither open the front storm door nor the windows. The snow had drifted so much, I could barely see the car in the driveway.

I became a bit nervous with the thought of “no way out.” There was very little activity on the highway.

In the meantime, I called my newspaper delivery girl and her mother who lived a few streets behind me to see how things were up there. They had shoveled themselves a few paths to the street. When I told them of my dilemma, they offered to come down—if they could get through the snow—and give me a path to the street and clear the snow from my doors. I believe they came early the next morning; that was Thursday.

In the meantime, Yana had to stay another night at Mary Hardigan’s. He called early in the morning saying he would attempt to walk home. The roads in that area had been plowed to some extent. On his way, he saw a police car on the road. The officer stopped and asked him where he was headed. He was going in the same direction for a bit, so he took Yana as far as he could, which was very much appreciated. Yana then walked the rest of the way from Dedham. There were very few cars on the road. The girls came early that day to give us a path and release the doors. The path was there when Yana reached home. He was exhausted, but we were happy to be in each other’s arms again.

We spent the next few days shoveling snow, as did our neighbors. There was a bit more activity on the highway—people walking, some with sleds, even a horse-drawn sleigh, some heading for the Stop & Shop where deliveries were arriving. The pace was very relaxed, with strangers conversing where, under normal circumstances, most people would be in a rush and not stop to talk.

Finally, an announcement was made on the radio and TV, stating that cars left on Route 128 could be retrieved. It wasn’t an easy task. Yana walked part way, but those vehicles that were on the road were helpful, and he received several rides. When arriving at Route 128, if your car wasn’t close by, the state highway people drove the car owners along the road to find their cars since they had all been moved to allow for plowing.

Since Truman Highway was still not ready for normal traffic, a co-worker who lived nearby and I walked to work one day and someone picked us up when we were almost there. Once was enough for me!

On Monday morning, huge dump trucks (I had never seen such large trucks) arrived to take away the accumulated snow.

Front loaders were also there, lifting the snow into the trucks and finally made the highway look more normal. The workers were even kind enough to clear our driveway entrances of snow. Gradually, everything got back to normal for us. How fortunate, considering the many tragic results from this fierce blizzard.

Statistics on the blizzard revealed that three thousand cars and five hundred trucks were stopped, creating a ten-mile backup. This was caused, in part, by two tractor-trailer trucks that skidded and jack-knifed on Route 128 south near Route 138 in Milton/Canton, a familiar location to us here at Fuller Village. Winds were blowing up to seventy-nine miles per hour in the Boston area with much drifting. The storm lasted thirty-two hours and forty minutes and dropped 27.1 inches of snow. The week the state stood still—February 6 to 13, 1978. If my husband had left work about an hour earlier, we might not have experienced as much anxiety. He was stopped very close to the beginning of the massive backup that quickly accumulated.

The Storm of the Century

John T. Driscoll

On Monday morning, February 6, 1978, local weather forecasters announced that the National Weather Service (NWS) had issued a "Snow Watch" for southeastern New England. New Englanders are not intimidated by "Snow Watch" alerts, however, and no one was alarmed as light snow began to fall at about 7:00 AM. But they should have been alarmed! Motorists driving to work were advised to expect a total accumulation of up to six inches, with temperatures in the low thirties.

At the time the snow started falling heavily, I was attending a business meeting in the town of Weston, not far from the Turnpike Authority maintenance head-quarters. As Chairman of the Massachusetts Turnpike Authority, I was already very proud of our men, our equipment, and our ability to do our job—and do it well and quickly. We had the best snow equipment available. I'm not saying that from a bragging point of view; we planned it that way. A few months after I had been sworn in as the turnpike chairman by Massachusetts Governor Endicott "Chub" Peabody in 1964, we reviewed the age and condition of our snow equipment and developed a schedule to purchase the best snowplowing equipment available. We always operated on the theory that we were only as good as our weakest link.

For this snow event, I decided I would work from our maintenance headquarters and keep tabs on the activities of the authority's seven maintenance districts. Very quickly, it became apparent this storm was going to tie up traffic throughout the state, possibly including the turnpike. So the Turnpike Authority and its maintenance crews across the state got going quickly on the snow-storm, which was developing rapidly in the eastern and middle part of the state. We set up emergency tow-parking locations adjacent to the turnpike and made arrangements to get tow trucks out there. The cars and trucks that became snowbound and stuck in the middle of the highway were towed to those emergency parking lots.

The snow was so bad that Route 128, which encircles the city of Boston, was getting clogged with stuck cars, trucks, and huge eighteen-wheeler trailers that kept other vehicles from getting by, thus compounding the danger. The state highway department, which was responsible for Route 128, did not set up emergency parking areas or towing, and did not have the necessary equipment to keep up snowplowing operations.

We focused on the turnpike, however, wanting to ensure we got all of the abandoned vehicles off the turnpike as quickly as possible so as not to tie up a particular section that, in turn, could have closed down the whole turnpike. We operated under that plan throughout the blizzard which lasted nearly thirty-three hours, with a total accumulation of fifty-five inches and snowdrifts reaching as high as fifteen feet! During the storm, I traveled the eastern part of the state with our chief engineer, our maintenance engineer, and, occasionally, with the state police.

Monday night, I slept on a cot for a few hours in one of the offices of the maintenance building. When dawn broke on Tuesday morning, February 7, the snow, which had been falling throughout Monday and overnight, was continuing and continued all day—accumulating an average of one inch per hour according to the U.S. Weather Bureau. Now, the snow was being whipped into a frenzy by hurricane-force winds, gusting to seventy-three miles per hour in Boston, with a high of ninety-two miles per hour recorded in the Cape Cod coastal community of Chatham. The blizzard had overwhelmed the entire state, particularly in the east.

We continued to plow the turnpike to widen the highway and, particularly, to open up the various interchanges which are, in a certain sense, more difficult than straight plowing on the highway. However, you could not get off the turnpike onto the local connecting roads and highways due to the amount of snow that had accumulated on them. But the turnpike maintenance crew had done an exceptionally fine job of keeping the turnpike reasonably open.

It was impossible to imagine the devastation. The huge snowdrifts and sixteen-foot flood tide were the result of two diverse weather systems—one from the warm Gulf Stream air heading north, and the other from a pocket of cold Canadian air, heading south. They intersected, erupted, and then stalled over New England. The intensity of the storm caught both meteorologists and motorists by surprise!

Towering waves cresting to eighty feet, wreaked havoc on coastal communities and homes. More than two thousand homes were destroyed—and more than nine thousand were partially destroyed! The cost estimate to damaged and destroyed homes was a staggering $172,500,000! Inland, the snow fell to an accumulation of twenty-three inches in the first twenty-four hours.

As the snowdrifts piled up, motorists throughout the commonwealth became stranded, but none more so than in the eastern part of the state, and particularly Greater Boston. By Tuesday, more than three thousand cars, and five hundred trucks, including jackknifed tractor-trailers, were snowbound. An eight-mile stretch of Route 128 looked like one immense, snow-covered parking lot. Roadways became impassable, and thousands or vehicles were abandoned. There was no way of estimating how many persons were trapped inside their stranded vehicles, as snow piled up to their wheelwells, hoods, and even roofs.

Many people spent the entire first night in their cars. One woman remembered: "The snow was so deep around the car, I could only see the state trooper's boots outside my window as he approached!" One man remembered, "How grateful we were to be saved and alive!" But not everyone was so lucky; the "Great Blizzard of 1978" claimed fifty-four lives in New England, twenty-nine of those in Massachusetts.

By Tuesday afternoon, the Massachusetts Highway Department was calling our engineers looking for help; they needed as much help as they could get on Route 128. As darkness fell about 4:00 PM in the afternoon that day, we started to deliver the first of our heavy snowplow equipment to the state public works yard on Route 9 at the corner of Route 128—not very far from the turnpike.

I was present when the first of our equipment was delivered, and we observed that many of the state snow-removal vehicles in their yard were broken down in disrepair. As our equipment arrived, the state public works people looked at our equipment as though they were B-52s bombers. We made arrangements to get out onto Route 128, and began the long, tedious job. It would take more than a week to open up many of the roads in eastern Massachusetts.

We organized our equipment and set them in tandem. Although they had been working all night, we used our own drivers. We didn't want other people using our equipment because it was in such good shape, and we didn't want to sustain any damage or get into any disagreements with the state. We knew best how to handle and protect our own equipment.

The first team of snowplows started to go south on Route 128 because the snowdrifts were smaller. The engineers chose to travel south on the northbound lane of 128; from the information they had about the snowdrifts, they believed that would be the easiest lane to open up. In due course, we would open up the southbound lanes. We traveled along southbound, with my vehicle following some of the snow vehicles. Many workers were involved.

I can remember getting out of the car and approaching abandoned cars with a snowbrush and a broom and clearing windshields. Each time I cleared a windshield, I had the fear I might find someone who had died because they couldn't get out and just stayed there for protection. Fortunately, we didn't find anyone inside the vehicles. All had somehow managed to make their way to nearby neighborhoods and were taken in by local residents whose homes abutted Route 128.

In time, we completed the job on Route 128, opening it to vehicles. Every so many feet, we would open up part of the guardrail between the northbound and southbound sections. We would plow across the median strip to access 128-South, so the tow vehicles and snowplows could get across to the other side and start to get some of those cars and trucks out of there. I must say our people did an exceptional job of opening 128. I can't tell you exactly how long it took, but I can tell you it took a considerable amount of time, and a considerable amount of towing and plowing to get Route 128 opened.

Residents seeking the protection of emergency shelters numbered 17,000 while emergency workers evacuated another 10,000 persons! Hospitals required blood and medical supplies. Doctors and nurses had to reach the sick and injured. Shelters had to be stocked with survival items. Fire trucks and ambulances had to be assured access to emergencies in snow-bound communities. Food and fuel supplies were required in nursing homes, housing projects, colleges, and private homes. The Massachusetts Civil Defense Agency was charged with coordinating this enormous task. The National Guard mobilized 5,000 Guardsmen, joined by another 350 federal troops.

More than 3,300 pieces of heavy equipment were used in opening up 4,360 miles of highways. By the time the storm ended on Tuesday, February 7, history had been made: it was the most ferocious blizzard ever recorded in Massachusetts and the Northeast, and remains so to this day.

Following the end of the storm, schools, non-emergency businesses, and many roads were closed for six days. Clearly, the principal focus of our storm effort had to be on the opening of strategic roadways to allow critical rescue attempts to be made. We devoted the next four or five days to opening state roads. All of the roads in eastern Massachusetts approaching and within the city of Boston were buried in snow. All of our equipment, from one end of the turnpike to the other, was brought down to the Boston area. Not surprisingly, all this effort began to take its toll on the Turnpike Authority's maintenance workers. Shift adjustments were made as we tried to give each worker some much-needed rest.

Before we stopped helping the state, we had plowed Route 95 off of Route 128, and went all the way down to the Rhode Island line. We plowed Route 128 the opposite way to Route 2, and then toward Concord as far as the Concord prison. We also went to the North Shore and through the city of Lynn. We opened up the causeway that connects Lynn and Nahant. Next, we plowed Storrow Drive and Memorial Drive leading into Boston. In Boston itself, we cleared out Beacon Hill, up Beacon Street past the front of the statehouse. We ploughed nearby principal arteries like Tremont Street and Cambridge Street.

We opened up all of that area, enabling Boston to get back to business as quickly as possible. Before we finished, we even helped plough the runways at Logan Airport. I continued to travel with our men to these areas, and we would stop at various restaurants along the way for lunch or dinner. Even then, we kept our equipment running, with the state police watching over it.

When it was all added up, the estimated total cost of the havoc to the Massachusetts economy was $441 million! Indeed, it was the "Storm of the Century!" At the beginning of the storm, Governor Dukakis imposed a driving ban. No cars other than emergency vehicles were allowed to travel on any road. I think the ban on cars lasted five or six days. It might have been as much as a week. Each morning of this crisis, the governor would hold a press conference at the Metropolitan District Commission headquarters on Somerset Street in Boston.

I never sought credit for what we had accomplished as an organization. But I believe recognition by the Dukakis administration was warranted for what the Turnpike Authority had achieved. While the governor did express his appreciation to me once in private, the only commonwealth official who ever gave the Turnpike Authority any recognition was John Snedeker, chairman of the Metropolitan District Commission. He came to me each day of the crisis and thanked me for what we were doing and what we had done.

If the Turnpike Authority had gotten no praise whatsoever, I would still have ended up feeling as I did: extremely proud and pleased. I wanted to demonstrate to the citizens of Massachusetts what the Turnpike Authority could and did, in fact, accomplish. We rescued eastern Massachusetts and the greater metropolitan area of Boston from the paralyzing grip of the worst snowstorm to hit New England in the twentieth century!

Unintended Consequences

Betsy Buchbinder

A series of unintended consequences led my family to Milton and ultimately to Fuller Village in 2005. I can actually trace the start of the initial event as far back as 1954 when Saul and I were making plans to buy our first home. We lived at that time in Roxbury near Franklin Park, but the house we found was in Newton, Massachusetts. It was lovely and would have been perfect for our needs at that time. And since our family included my widowed mother who lived with us, we brought her to see the house before we signed any legal documents. She agreed that the house was just wonderful but...

My mother belonged to what she called a "bridge club" with five of her widowed friends. In reality, "bridge club" was a euphemism for what it really was: a poker club. The ladies met every Saturday evening, had dinner in each other's home, and then played cards. They all lived either in Mattapan, Dorchester, or Roxbury—all within an easy taxi drive to one another. Our intended move to Newton was, for her, totally unacceptable!

Having agreed with us that the house was lovely, I clearly remember how she coyly asked if I would promise to drive her to her club meetings every Saturday at five o'clock, and would Saul agree to pick her up after the game at about eleven? Every Saturday evening! And thus began the search for another place to call home.

I remember thinking that the town of Milton would be the ideal solution. How could I not have realized that before? For a fifty cent taxi cab ride, my mother could continue playing cards each and every Saturday evening while Saul and I could make our own Saturday evening plans. Our move to Milton kept the "bridge club" intact.

As a result of our move to Milton, our children started kindergarten at the Tucker School. I so admired the faculty and principal that I applied to teach there and subsequently taught at my beloved Tucker School for twenty-five years until I retired.

My adult life has been enriched by our move to Milton and by my becoming an active part of the fabric of the community. It was while I served on the executive board of Milton Residences for the Elderly that I became aware of a plan to create Fuller Village about two miles from where we lived on Vose Hill Road. I viewed the projected plans at almost all of the monthly meetings of MRE and was thrilled to see the plans become reality. With little effort, I convinced my husband that this is where we should move. From the city of Newton to the town of Milton via a Saturday night poker club decision was a circuitous route that became a winning hand!

When Saul saw the initial plans for Fuller Village, he agreed with me that this was a remarkable project being planned and that, by moving here, we could remain in the community we loved. I could remain a Milton Town Meeting member, remain with MRE, and continue to represent Milton on the board of South Shore Elder Services. The bonus for both of us has been our life style within Fuller Village and the wonderful services it has provided us.

Unintended consequences led Saul and me to Milton and, serendipitously, to Fuller Village. In reading the ninety stories produced by our memoir project, *We Remember When*, you have "met" the remarkable folk who have become our dear friends and neighbors.

Fuller Village in Milton, Massachusetts

INDEX

If you would like to know more about Fuller Village,
you are cordially invited to visit Fuller's website,
www.FullerVillage.org
or call 617-361-7900 for further information.

LaVergne, TN USA
23 March 2011
221341LV00003B/3/P